It's Not Rocket Science, It's Parenthood!

Effective and witty ways to deal with the lunacy of parenthood.

Shannon D. Jackson

It's Not Rocket Science,

It's Parenthood!

Shannon D. Jackson

Edited by J.K. Kelley

Published by KCCOLLABORATIVE
Copyright © 2013 by KCCOLLABORATIVE

Copyright © 2013 by KCCOLLABORATIVE

All rights reserved. No part of this book may be used or reproduced in any form or by any means, electronic or mechanical, including photocopying, recording, or by any information storage and retrieval systems, without written permission of the publisher or author, except where permitted by law.

Please note that much of this publication reflects the author's personal experience, is meant to entertain, and is not intended to replace medical advice. Although the author and publisher have made every reasonable attempt to achieve complete accuracy of the content in this guide, they assume no responsibility for errors or omission. You should use this information as you see fit, and at your own risk. Your particular situation may not be exactly suited to the examples illustrated here; in fact, it's likely that they won't be the same, and you should adjust your use of the information and recommendations accordingly.

EBooks are not transferable. They cannot be sold, shared, or given away as it is an infringement on the copyright of this work. Please respect the rights of the author and do not file share.

Published by
KCCOLLABORATIVE
Website: itsnotrocketsciencepeople.com
Printed by KCCOLLABORATIVE LLC
Printed in the United States
First Edition

Edited by J.K. Kelley
Proofread by Jackie Getz

ISBN 978-0-9886281-0-6

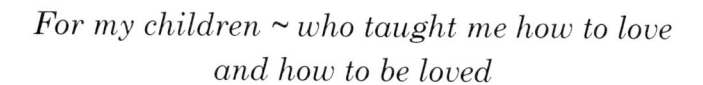

*For my children ~ who taught me how to love
and how to be loved*

For my husband ~ forever, minus one day

Acknowledgements

I would like to give special thanks to my husband, sister, the girls from liquid therapy, the beautiful girl who lives in the basement, and the J man. Without all of whom this literary masterpiece would not have come to fruition. Your enthusiasm, guidance, criticisms, and unending support are greatly appreciated. I am so fortunate to have such a great mismatch of personalities to call my own.

I also would like to acknowledge the amazing abilities of J.K. Kelley, editorial guru. He has the amazing ability to cure adverbial conjuctivitis. As well as proofreader/second editor, Jackie Getz, for going above and beyond.

TABLE OF CONTENTS

INTRODUCTION..1

THIS IS NOT YOUR EVERYDAY
GUIDEBOOK..5

TODDLERS..17

ACKNOWLEDGEMENTS
AND REWARDS...35

THE BENEFITS OF SELF-CONTROL.............41

PERFECTION...51

STOP TAKING THEIR CRAP
SO PERSONALLY..69

THE PITFALLS OF FAVORITISM...................77

RESPECT..91

UNGRATEFULNESS GETS YOU
NOTHING..103

TIMEOUT CAN HAPPEN ANYWHERE........111

LOSER LOSER 121

LESSONS IN BOREDOM............................129

NOSES TOUCHING 137

THE ART OF SENTENCE
WRITING...143

TAKE ALL THE TIME YOU NEED................151

YOU TEACH PEOPLE HOW TO
TREAT YOUR SIBLING....................................157

TRASH TALKING AND TENACITY...............167

MOMMY WORDS AND TEA
PARTIES...175

SNEAKING OUT..183

BULLIES...189

SKIPPING SCHOOL 201

SMOKING AND FRIENDS 213

SEX, DRUGS, AND ROCK-N-ROLL 221

MENDING FENCES...237

PARENTING IS A MARATHON.....................245

CHAPTER ONE:

INTRODUCTION

INTRODUCTION

Do you remember how, right after you had that first baby, you would sit and stare at her, waiting for a blink? How you'd call everyone close to you, friend or family, and talk about how she was the most precious baby ever? We all have thousands of those moments: the first smile, the first word, the first step, the hugs and kisses. This book isn't about those moments.

This book is about all the other moments. The moments when you're lying awake wondering where you went wrong with that precious little baby. The moments when you really start weighing the key question: set up a college fund, or place an attorney on retainer? This book is about the long, hard, exhausting journey we take as parents.

Parenting forced me to develop some very unconventional methods for coping with the long post baby challenge of raising children. At some point, after the cute baby blinks, and before you decide to check yourself into the psych ward you have to develop some coping mechanisms. You need to cultivate your sense of humor, strap on your hip waders, and think outside-the-box. This book will help you do that, and don't worry; it's not rocket science, it's parenthood.

CHAPTER TWO:

THIS IS NOT YOUR EVERYDAY GUIDEBOOK

THIS IS NOT YOUR EVERYDAY GUIDEBOOK

This book is not a professional resource for any childhood medical or psychological disorder. I am not a doctor, psychologist, or counselor. I do not have a parenting TV show and I have never been a super nanny. This is not your typical 'how to be a better parent' guidebook. You will not learn any amazing tricks on how to raise future doctors and lawyers. I have no secrets on how to make your child a genius. None of my children (I have three of the little darlings) could read by eight months of age. This book is for all of you parents who feel overwhelmed, worn out and just plain disappointed. Parenthood was supposed to make you happy. You had all these fantasies about what a great family you'd have. You would have movie nights filled with popcorn and laughter. You dreamed about board game marathons lasting into the wee hours of the night. You hoped for long, meaningful conversations where you could impart your wisdom to the fruit of your loins. Your beautiful little beings would be brilliant. All of their teachers were going to point to them as examples for the rest of the class to follow. Neighbors were going to want your perfect children to play with their sadly flawed children so some of the perfection could rub off. You would have darling little angels, leading the choir with their little cherub voices.

Didn't happen? It didn't happen for me either. Parenthood is rarely what we bargained for. The perfect fantasy family somehow turned into a hard hat work zone. Parenthood is work. It's overwhelming, exhausting, thankless hard work. We make so many sacrifices, and not only do these little beings not recognize all that we give up, nor shower us with eternal gratitude, but they fundamentally don't care! In fact, the more you give, the more they expect.

Parenthood is humiliating. You thought it was embarrassing when they were three and screaming the whole time you shopped for groceries? Wait until the school calls you because your wretched thirteen-year-old informed the science teacher that he's a moron. Try convincing the vice principal that you raised him to be respectful, when the vice principal informs you that your child addresses him as "Dude."

Then there is the worry, so much worry. From morning till night, we are concerned about our children. Are they happy? Are they healthy? Are they doing well in school? Do they any have friends? Do they have good friends? Will they make varsity? Will they even make the team? Does that require stitches? What constitutes a head injury? What am I doing wrong? Every single day brings worries old and new.

Worry runs neck and neck with guilt. You've had the worst day at work, you have to take the dog to the vet, your mom has called three times, you're out of milk, you still have homework to guide, and then you lash out at the precious little boy who just wrapped himself around your leg. Guilt consumes you. Why did I say that? Why wasn't I more patient? How will this affect his self-esteem?

Will he complain about this to his therapist when he's thirty?

Some, perhaps many of you, may now be sitting in comfy chairs thinking: "Holy shit! I'm not the only one? Other parents are overwhelmed? Other parents are clueless as to what they're doing? Other parents are keeping themselves up at night wondering about all the different ways they're screwing up their kid?" Yup. You are part of a large majority, not the minority.

Are you still having trouble believing? I'll make it clearer. People lie. They stand back, plaster on those fake smiles, and swear that there isn't a better job on the planet. Really? In the first place, some job: you not only don't get paid, you pay to keep it. Doesn't it make you wonder if those people are closet drinkers? If I was half crocked, I probably wouldn't notice if the boys were dying the cat blue. I wouldn't care if the school called because my child forgot to wear socks (fifth time this month). I could rationalize the nutritional value of eating popcorn for dinner at least three nights a week. I certainly wouldn't be as tired; I would be able to pass out every night, instead of lying awake consumed with worry and guilt.

Are they delusional, these parents, who think this is so easy? How do they do it? Here's the truth: they don't. They probably aren't closet drinkers, and they're not setting out to deceive. They're simply in denial, and you can imagine why. What would that say about them, as parents and people, if their kids were not perfect? This is supposedly the most important job they will ever have, and they are screwing it up? If their identity is so tied up in how "good" their kids are, then they can't admit when the kids are "naughty" because that must make them bad parents. Who wants to feel like a huge failure at the one job everyone else seems to do competently?

Why do that to yourself? Labeling yourself a failure is unkind and unfair to yourself. Children are naughty little beings. That is the nature of growing up. It's a learning process. We learn from our experiences. We learn when we make mistakes. The perfect parents don't exist, though some people put on a pretty good front to make it seem that way. So take a deep breath and relax, because your family is normal. Yup, they are. Hold onto this: you are not the only parent on the planet wondering, what the hell happened? Where are the movie nights? Why does carving pumpkins with your little monsters give you a headache? Why do other parents brag about what great friends their kids are, while yours are plotting each others' murders? Is it possible to die from exhaustion?

The truth is that parenthood is a ceaseless, messy, thankless, expensive, and exhausting process. And for every moment that makes you wonder if the insanity will ever stop, there are a hundred moments that leave you with that tingly 'this is love' feeling. They really are the greatest part of us. All we need to do now is figure out methods of creating more of those tingly 'I love being a parent' moments. We can do this. If we can learn to be honest, cut out the bullshit, step up to the plate, and do what works, we can create the families we desire.

Growing up should be viewed as a learning process. If you can accept that your precious little bundle of energy is constantly in the process of learning, it will change your attitude towards naughty behavior. And yes, your little angel is naughty. They are all naughty: yours, mine, and some more than others. If they were perfect, they would be little adults…except that we're not perfect either! If you understand that they are not being naughty on purpose, that they have to learn how to behave, then you can look at naughtiness as part of growing up. Yep, your wretched little guy is absolutely normal. He just needs to learn a better way to behave. More effective parenting techniques will teach him that better behavior.

The first step is to learn how and why discipline is essential to the happy family outcome. I firmly believe that consistent discipline is key to creating a more peaceful environment. You might be thinking: discipline is unpleasant, so how can I have a peaceful house by adding unpleasantness?

Because consistency teaches our children that we mean what we say. Our children will not continue behaviors that result in unwanted outcomes. The more consistent your disciplinary measures, the fewer disciplinary measures you will have to carry out.

CHAPTER THREE:

TODDLERS

TODDLERS

Toddlers are the people that will kill you! Yup, I know they're cute, with their fat little bodies and dimply little smiles. They have those contagious little giggles. They still have so much babyness about them. I love how they curl up in little balls when they sleep and how warm and cuddly they are when they wake up. However, they are capable of killing you because they never stop. They never stop!

You wake up exhausted because, contrary to what the books say, your child still wakes up at night. You then drink two cups of cold coffee, because the small person clinging to your leg wants: love, breakfast, her toy, more love, down off her chair, up in her chair, down off her chair, up in her chair, etc. After you put a stop to breakfast (even though she only ate twelve cereal flakies), you put on an educational toddler program so you could clean up the 148 cereal flakies she left on the chair, table, floor, and wall. Then you do the dishes while she destroys the living room. While you clean the living room, she destroys the kitchen. You clean the (pick a disaster area), while she destroys the (pick a new disaster area). This repeats itself in millions of homes, all across the Western world, and probably the rest of it as well, millions of times a day. Multiply that by two or more for those of us who decided to have another baby, so that first one wouldn't be lonely.

I'm not saying that parenting a toddler lacks rewards. After that long frustrating day, when your toddler puts her little arms around your neck, and hugs you with that trachea-crushing hug, it's not oxygen deprivation that makes your heart sing—it's love! And yet, even with all the beautiful moments your little luvbug brings, at the end of the day, you still drop in bed at night utterly exhausted. And you'll get up tomorrow and do it all again, because exhaustion doesn't negate our responsibilities. We still have to parent. Don't lose hope, because we can make it better. I did, so I know you can.

My oldest is a boy. He was a perfect baby in every way; fat, happy and slept all the time. As a fearful new mom, I took him to the doctor because my friends' babies didn't sleep all the time. My doctor collected my copay and told me to consider myself lucky. I did. And then, my tiny narcoleptic grew into a stubborn, strong-willed toddler. You've heard of the terrible twos; my little bundle of love started at a terrible one and a half. When my son was eighteen months old, my husband came home one evening to find me crying on the porch. I had changed my mind. I didn't really want to be a parent anymore. All I felt was exhaustion and frustration. Given that I was pregnant with my second child, these weren't exactly the ideal feelings to be having.

It didn't matter how many times I told, scolded, pleaded, explained and/or begged. My son did whatever he wanted. In my frustration, I began yelling all the time. It wasn't a great time for our family. I was this young, overwhelmed mother. He was this normal, out-of-control toddler. Our home felt more like a war zone than the peaceful safe haven it was supposed to be.

And then someone gave me a book. Amid the various battles in the First Toddler War, I managed to read it. This insightful book made me realize that yelling, which was my basic method of parenting, was ineffective. It helped me acknowledge that yelling was damaging to our little people. It helped me understand that I was really yelling because I didn't want to discipline my precious baby. I wanted him to mind me, but I wanted to avoid the guilt of discipline. When I accepted that the yelling wasn't working and that the discipline I was threatening (the timeout, the loss of the toy, etc.) was unavoidable, I could stop yelling. The book proved correct, and I stopped yelling altogether.

Much like you, faithful reader, I read a lot of books. I hate to admit it, but I don't recall the name of the above mentioned literary masterpiece. That's not important, though. What I want to convey to you is the value of not yelling, and the idea that you can accomplish huge changes in behavior without yelling.

So here is your first lesson: STOP YELLING.

For example, instead of yelling twenty times to "stop throwing your cereal flakies on the floor," I say in a calm, normal tone, "I said to not throw cereal flakies on the floor, so I guess you're done." Remove the cereal-chucker from the cereal flakies and say again, "I said to not throw cereal flakies on the floor so I guess you're done. We'll give it a try again later and see if you can listen." This really does work. I did it. My son didn't starve. By the time he was thirteen, he measured out at a formidable 6'2" and 200 lbs. It would be reasonable for you to think:

"If I remove my child from the cereal flakies, he will have a fit." You'd be right. He will. Mine certainly did. He was used to getting what he wanted. He was mad. He yelled and cried, throwing himself on the floor. I calmly stepped around him. I did not yell. I repeated that we do not throw cereal flakies, and left him crying on the floor. After he calmed down, I asked if he would like to try again. He did! For two minutes, he sat and ate his cereal flakies. Then he smiled his wonderful little smile, looked me in the eye, and threw his cereal flakies on the floor.

As frustrating as this is, it is very normal for your child to test his limits. If he has had his way since he entered this world, he doesn't believe that you mean what you say. You will have to prove it to him. So, reread the above paragraphs and follow the steps. Don't lose hope; after you are consistent about not throwing cereal flakies, he will eventually stop throwing them. He will eventually even stop throwing fits about cereal flakies. I am sorry to inform you, however, that he will not stop throwing fits. He will simply not throw fits about cereal flakies because his cereal-related fit-throwing didn't gain him anything. Everytime he threw cereal flakies, he got exactly the same result: removal from the cereal.

I had a friend who put her kid's high chair over a shower curtain so the cleanup would be easier. Do you want to be that parent? Wouldn't it be great to be the parent of the kid who can eat at a restaurant without having to apologize for the mess she made under the table? It is possible. Ask your waitress. She has waited on both types of kids. No matter how nice she was about your little food-throwing demoness, she doesn't appreciate the mess. Practice daily, at home, the behavior you want your child to model, and you won't be embarrassed in public.

Before we continue, I'd like to emphasize something. I rely upon you, fellow parent or future fellow parent, to use common sense throughout this book. It is fine and wise to modify, expand, twist, or stretch any of the ideas in this book to fit your child's specific personality and needs. Each child is fundamentally different. If your child cries simply because you spoke harshly to him or her, you must soften your approach. I hope you modify these ideas accordingly. If your child is extremely difficult, then I challenge you to find effective ways of changing his behavior without damaging who he is. In the previous example, hopefully you see that I am not advocating that you starve your child. The lesson is about not throwing food on the floor, which is why you remove the toddler and allow for another chance later.

And that leads into your second lesson: BE CONSISTENT.

You have to be consistent. If you say it, you must mean it. You don't have to yell to get the behavior you want; you simply have to follow through on what you say. If you do this from the beginning of your little bundle of joy's life, you will not have to battle him when he's three. However, if you're starting from three, don't worry. It'll be a little more work, but you'll make it. Since you already signed on for the eighteen year program, you have no choice but to follow through. Parenthood isn't for the lazy. It will be exhausting initially, but so is having an out-of-control toddler. If life's going to be hell for a while anyway, why not have it a hell where you get a benefit at some point, namely a new behavior pattern?

The importance of consistency applies to everything in the daily life of your child. Your children must learn at the earliest possible age that you mean what you say. If your child screams in the grocery cart and you let him out, he will scream every time he wants out, because it works for him. However, if you ignore him and just continue shopping, he will eventually stop screaming. Maybe not the first time (if his screaming has worked previously), maybe not the fifth time (if he is extremely stubborn), but eventually he will stop. Yes, I know people are looking. They are undoubtedly whispering about your screaming child. It's very embarrassing. I know you want to pack up your little screamer and go home. You can live without toilet paper, can't you?

Parenthood is a lesson in humiliation. Get used to it. It is more important for your child to learn how to behave in public, including the acceptance of riding in a grocery cart, than it is for you to worry about what the Wally World shoppers think of you.

Think of your little luvbug as a gambler at heart. Because you haven't been very consistent, because sometimes you were too tired, busy, distracted, or you just didn't really mean what you threatened, you didn't follow through. Every time you didn't, he won that hand. Over time, our precious little gamblers understand that sometimes they can get away with it, so it's worth placing the bet. They roll the dice and see if today is the day the house (parent) wins, or if today is the day they (little gamblers) win. By being consistent, your little card shark will learn that he loses every time. He will soon learn that it isn't a fun game to play. The cost is too high.

Let's move on, pretending for now that your child has mastered the basic principle of sitting in the cart without a banshee wail. It is imperative that you acknowledge that good behavior. I truly believe that children want to be good. It's easier for them. The people around them are happier and more loving. When your child is good, she is easier to love. You want to hug and kiss her, throw her in the air, spin her around in circles. When she's screaming at the top of her lungs, you're one step away from deserting her with the tomatoes and pretending that someone else owns her. Thus, after you have shown your child that you mean what you say, when she understands that it is easier for her to follow your instructions because you will follow through with the consequences, you must reward and acknowledge her good behavior. Positive reinforcement is essential at this point.

While children are all individuals; some eager to please, some abrasive. I firmly believe that deep down, they all have the same desire to be good. They are not born knowing how to do that. It is our job as their parents to teach them. Your little guy doesn't understand that screaming in the store is not acceptable and will not get him the desired results. He thinks screaming will get him down. However, after he learns that you mean what you say, and he sits quietly while you shop, if you tell him how proud you are of him and give him a reward, he will learn very quickly to behave. He will come to crave that positive reinforcement from you. He wants to make you happy. He wants to make you proud. He wants to feel that love from you. This is a great time to ask him if it feels good to behave. You have to help him make the connection that he has control over that feeling of being good. He makes that happen for himself by following your expectations. The reward can be anything you think would help prompt the desired behavior. It could be a sticker, a piece of gum, a hug, or a high-five. If you have a little people pleaser in your cart, it may only take a few words describing how proud you are of him. At this age children are beginning to discover what they can control in their worlds, and this works because it feeds into that. They learn that they can manipulate their situation and 'win' by behaving well.

CHAPTER FOUR:

ACKNOWLEDGMENTS AND REWARDS

ACKNOWLEDGEMENTS AND REWARDS

We keep a prize box in our home. I fill it with small things that I think my children, and my nieces and nephews would like. When they meet my expectations, they can choose something out of the prize box. I use the prize box to motivate them in a multitude of different ways. If they do a particularly good job on a task, they can pick out a treasure from the prize box. If they do something unexpected, like picking up their room without being asked, they can claim a treat from our prize box. Maybe they get caught displaying kindness to one of their siblings; they can choose something out of the prize box. It still amazes me how much cleaning I can get in return for the surplus plastic spiders I picked up after Halloween.

I heard a parent once say that they were not willing to reward their child for meeting basic standards. I don't understand that. As adults, we receive regular rewards for our good behavior. Your boss tells you that you did a good job, maybe even gives you a raise. You met all of your diet goals, so you reward yourself with those new shoes you've been coveting. Your sister tells you that you're her best friend because you are always there for her. I want my child to feel that the energy they put into being good is benefiting them. It is not going unnoticed or unappreciated.

Having children of different ages, we have different bedtimes in our home. For example, the ten-year-old goes to bed first, followed by the fifteen-year-old a bit later, and then lastly the seventeen-year-old. Our littlest bed bug constantly begs to stay up later. In order for him to stay up a bit longer, we developed a system so he can earn the right to stay up. If he reads at some point during the day, I will match minute for minute (up to 30 minutes) in delayed nighty-night time. He is rewarded for reading by staying up later. If he doesn't read, he goes to bed at the normal time. Isn't this similar to your going to work every day? If you go to work, you get paid. If you don't work, you don't get paid.

Perhaps the parent who doesn't acknowledge and reward their child reasons that the child will learn to behave only when a reward is in play. That isn't the case. If you balance discipline with rewards, eventually you will not have to discipline or reward. After your little one masters the discipline/reward cycle on basic behavior issues, new versions of it will apply that are relevant to their later stages of development. Your child will move on to other things. My fifteen-year-old does not need a sucker to be good in the store. She needs discipline and rewards for different, more age appropriate things. For example, because she is older, every A on her report card gets her $10.00, every B gets her $5.00, and C's get her nothing because I am not paying her to be average. But there's more. For every D she brings home, she pays me $5.00, and for every F she pays me $10.00! Now that is a perfect example of the discipline and reward system for children who are in school. We will obviously not be continuing that system through college.

CHAPTER FIVE:

THE BENEFITS OF SELF-CONTROL

THE BENEFITS OF SELF-CONTROL

What if I happen to have that super stubborn child who knows better and yet continues to repeat the naughty behavior over and over again? Let's use the example of hitting. Your cute little toddler, dressed in her cute little dress, with her cute little pigtails, repeatedly hits you and/or anyone else when she's unhappy. She knows she can't behave this way. She's not a slow learner, as a matter of fact; your little genius can already read three letter words. She does not need to learn what is good and what is bad. She needs a lesson in self-control.

Self-control is at the core of every behavioral issue. Self-control is vital to our children's success as people, yet we never talk about it that way. We say, "oh, little Jon-Jon has anger problems," or "Katie is a biter." Bullshit. That is just naming the behavior without solving it. What I see in little Jon-Jon or Katie is a lack of self-control. I understand it, and you probably do as well, for you and I were both four years old once upon a time. When you're four years old, it feels really good to hit someone when you're angry. However, it is not acceptable, and shows a lack of self-control. If the four-year-old chooses to do it anyway, I can help her learn self-control through consistent discipline. If little Jon-Jon has to stand in the corner every time he hits his little sister, hitting his little sister will lose its appeal. If Katie has to bite a sponge soaked in vinegar every time she bites someone, she will eventually stop biting.

Recently I was watching one of those reality police shows. The episode featured a seven-year-old boy who had locked his mom out of the house. He refused the policeman's repeated request to open the door. After gaining permission from the mom, the policeman broke a window to gain entrance into the house. After the policeman dragged the delinquent child out from under the bed, they placed him on the couch where he immediately started kicking his mother. Seriously! But guess what he didn't do: kick the policeman. Even when the policeman intervened on the mother's behalf, Junior didn't kick the cop. He knew there would be serious consequences if he even came close to kicking the policeman. At that moment,

Junior demonstrated the capacity for self-control.

My son had a friend who would have a fit whenever it was time to leave. His mom and I agonized over this. We labeled it for him: he had trouble with transitions. We talked with him over and over, and reminded him that he would get to come back. We hugged him and wiped off his tears. We dug him out from behind the couch and promised him that if he left like a good boy, then he could come back even sooner. We did this every time he came over. One day his mom couldn't come to pick him up, so she sent his dad. When his dad said it was time to go, this little traumatized boy who had 'trouble with transitions' grabbed his coat and climbed into the car without a single tear. I was shocked. Do you see what happened? He chose to exercise self-control at that moment because he knew his dad wouldn't tolerate the fit. No excuses, no drama. Just get in the car and go. So much for labeling the behavior.

Instead of labeling the behaviors, thus in a sense giving our children excuses for why they do these things, we need to teach them self-control. It doesn't really matter why you're doing whatever you're doing. It just matters that you stop doing it. A mom once explained to me that her four-year-old would bite her little sister because she was jealous. Really? Jealous? Call me insensitive, but I don't care. I know that her being jealous matters to her mom, but it certainly doesn't matter to her little sister. Isn't it far more logical to teach her that being jealous does not give you the right to bite someone? Especially your baby sister? That mom has the opportunity to teach her daughter self-control. By being consistent, her green-eyed monster will learn that biting is not okay; that she can and will exercise self-control, or she will have to bite a sponge soaked in vinegar. Later, when she's a little older, she will learn how to deal appropriately with jealousy.

If you stop offering excuses for your child's misdeeds, you can help them develop self-control. This concept is huge, people. It is one of the most important things you will learn in this book. Learning to control their own behavior in terms of reactions and impulses is key to becoming a successful human being. This is essential because you will not be allowed to follow your child throughout their adulthood explaining away their bad behavior.

So be consistent, stop offering excuses, acknowledge their good behavior, and focus on teaching self-control. As you read this book, you may not agree with my chosen methods of discipline. Some people believe in spankings; some people don't. Some kids respond well to some forms of discipline, some kids don't. If Katie, the teeth impression artist, loves vinegar, then lemon juice would probably be a better choice. Here is what I want you to understand: whatever discipline measures (spankings, timeouts, etc.) you implement in your family, you must be consistent to be effective.

CHAPTER SIX:

PERFECTION

PERFECTION

I come as your liberator. I herewith liberate you from the idea of perfection. Parenthood is difficult enough without requiring perfection from your children or yourself. In fact, if you're demanding perfection from your child, stop! Your child has enough to deal with without you adding perfection to their list. It's tough to be a kid. It's tougher than when we were kids. At least we could draw pictures of guns in first grade. Your future artist can't do that in today's world. We could dress up for Halloween and parade around the school showing off our costumes. Not anymore; it's not politically correct. Our kids have to deal with hormones, peer pressure, social stresses, academic pressures, even crazy ass drugs that require household and farm chemicals to manufacture. They don't need perfection too.

What if we expected improvement rather than perfection? What if we allowed for mistakes, even relapses, of certain behaviors? Try to think of your child like an employee in training. You patiently explain your company's policies, and for every new concept you introduce, you allow for a certain period of adjustment. As the CEO of your company, you expect misunderstandings, mistakes, and confusion for new trainees. That's why they are in training. However, since we are talking about our progeny, the comparison breaks down at a certain point. You can't fire your kid for unpardonable mistakes. Because we have to keep our little familial employees, we must find effective ways of teaching and motivating them to get the results we desire.

Let's use the example of lying. Yes, your precious little gem lies. They all lie. I actually had a parent profess to me once that his child never lies. What a fool. All children lie. Lying is a natural response in children. They connect rather quickly with the idea that they can avoid trouble if they can convince you that they didn't do it, take it, touch it, eat it, or say it. More importantly, they can get their little brother in trouble by saying he did it. Smart little monkeys.

By accepting that your little imperfect person will lie, you are able to see it as simply another lesson that you must impart to your charming little perjurer. There are two lessons that I want my children to understand about lying: that I am not an idiot, and that lying is a character issue. My standard response when one of my little storytellers is caught lying is: "Although it insults me that you think I believe this crap, lying is a character issue. Lying says a lot about your character right now. Obviously you need to work on your character. So, I guess you need to write sentences."

Writing sentences is a great form of discipline because it reinforces your lesson and, as a bonus, works on penmanship and vocabulary. Sentences in my house are not short. I do not want "I am sorry" fifty times. Sentences in my house are long and time-consuming. I want: "I will try not to lie because I am a person of good character. Lying undermines trust. And although I thought my mom was dumb enough to believe me, she has proven me wrong. I will develop good character and try not to lie."

The next time (and there will be a next time) your precious little hugbug lies, repeat the above statement and increase the sentences. Keep this technique age appropriate. If your child is younger, he can start with three to five sentences, increasing by one or two with each repeated transgression. If your child is older, he can start with more sentences, increased by increments of five or ten. Remember, we are striving for improvement here, not perfection. Stop being so angry at your cute little fantasy author and remind yourself that parenthood is ongoing and repetitive. Trust that by being consistent, your child will eventually get tired of the discipline, and stop behaving in unacceptable ways. If every time he lies, your little falsifier has to write the above sentences, he will lie less.

Now for you, as the parent, stop beating

yourself up for not being perfect. Your child does not need a perfect parent. They don't need homemade cookies or flawlessly made Halloween costumes. They don't need meals made from scratch every night. What they do require is the knowledge that you love them, unconditionally, no matter what, even when they're naughty—especially then. This is so crucial because believing that their parents love them is at the core of how your children feel about themselves. It defines the people they will become. If you feel, as a child, that your own mother or father doesn't love you, how could anyone else love you? Further, if you are unlovable, then why care about yourself or others? Think for a minute about what that could mean. It is imperative that your children know that you love them.

Now we are back to the worry, huh? I know you love your children. It's why you're reading this book, perhaps one of many such books you've read. You know, and I believe, that you love your children. But here is the important question that only you and your child can answer: does your child feel loved by you? Knowing it yourself is not enough. What matters is what your child feels. Does your child feel loved by you? Or, because of ineffective parenting, does your child feel like a disappointment who can't do anything right, and is always in trouble?

The first thing to get clear in your mind is that effective discipline will give your child the tools and self-control to make the needed changes. This, followed by positive reinforcement, will make your child feel successful and want to make the necessary changes. If your child is constantly in trouble, for the same issues, with no improvement, then your discipline measures are not working.

Secondly, it is essential that you tell your children daily that you love them. That you are so lucky to have them; they are wonderful, creative, funny, and smart. When my youngest was eight years old, he loved that he was tall. Because he loved to hear it, we told him how tall he was all the time. Our children need us to say those things to them. They need to be showered with affection. They need to be hugged, kissed, and cuddled. If you think your child knows that you love him even though you don't say it, you are wrong. Make yourself say it. Every day. Even to that difficult child, the one that you're ready to strangle. If you are just so damn angry because it seems like he never gives you a break, then make yourself hug him anyway. Especially him. He really needs to know that you love him.

I have that difficult child, the one that is so daunting because he is so wretched. At the end of the day, after a thousand battles, you're not sure if you actually like him, let alone want to shower him with affection. Looking back, I think he got up every morning with the goal of making me prove that I loved him. Sometimes I didn't succeed in proving it to him. Sometimes I could hardly look at him. My parenting techniques were completely ineffective. I didn't have any help. I was so critical of myself and of him. I wanted him to be perfect, and he constantly refused me. And then, one day, I had an experience that changed my views on perfection.

I had a friend who was perfect. Her house was perfect. Her children were perfect. They were always quiet. They were always clean. They didn't have tantrums. Despite her perfection, we were friends. Once we took all our kids to the mall. As we were walking toward the entrance, a giant mud puddle blocked our path. My wild boy ran and jumped right in the middle of it. Mud splashed everywhere, covering his shoes, up his legs. He stood there in the middle of that mud puddle and laughed. I was mortified. He was being imperfect again. He really wasn't trying to be naughty, though. He is the kind of kid who sees adventure everywhere. He is fun and impulsive and brave. My friend's daughter looked up at her mom with that hopeful look only a young child has when she longs to experience the same childlike delight of another. Her mom, to my horror, quietly said, "Good girls don't get dirty." It was a lightning moment of clarity for me: having perfect children does not make you a perfect parent. How horrible for that girl to believe that she will not be a good girl if she gets dirty. Children get dirty! That's part of childhood. How awesome for my naughty, impulsive, imperfect boy to feel the joy that comes from doing something crazy and spontaneous, like jumping into a mud puddle. How lucky he is, not to have someone engrave lasting damage into his character, such as the foolish idea that good kids don't get dirty! I wish I could say I had all this figured out prior to the mud splash, but I didn't. The realization hit me, stuck, and left my thinking forever changed.

Some kids are more difficult than others. Some have to learn every lesson the hard way. Sometimes, even though we want to save our children grief and pain by telling them what we know, they have to learn it for themselves. They are demanding and exhausting. No matter what we do, they fight us. They are a thankless lot, these kids. But stick with it, be consistent, and love them anyway.

Some kids are just easier, and I also have one of those. My sweetest little plum demonstrates this perfectly. He is just the kindest little guy ever. I was at a dinner party once and my friend, who doesn't have any children, was observing all these crazy kids causing mayhem. Now my super sweet little three-year-old is perched on my knee, keenly watching the mayhem unfolding. My friend turns to me and asks me how I get him to sit perfectly because she wants her future child to mimic that behavior. I laughed and explained that he wouldn't get down. My little guy is an observer. He isn't the brave little guy in the middle of all the excitement. He is content to simply sit back and watch. He is easy and always ready to please. If I had only had him, I would think very highly of my parenting abilities. Taken solo, he makes me look like a parental rock star.

That would be fiction. I have two older children, and neither one would have sat contentedly on my lap. One being a boy and the other being a girl, they come with their own unique challenges. My firstborn was a puddle-stomping tornado who destroyed everything in his path. We could almost keep track of him on the Weather Channel. When he was a toddler, there were days when we didn't leave the house. Seriously. If he was having a bad day, I didn't make a quick trip to the store. This was in the days when my parenting techniques were a total failure. My daughter, super cute and usually pretty easy going, hated strangers. She was very shy and clingy. Strangers would approach us to comment on how adorable she was, and she would cry. Every time. She didn't like group activities like weddings. I spent the entirety of a dear friend's wedding in the parking lot, watching cars drive by. Every time I would get her calmed down enough to return, she would cry upon entering the building.

I hope every parent has the difficult kid in varying degrees. This kid makes you work, keeps you awake at night—but also reminds you not to judge. This is a tough concept because we are a judgmental lot. When we see a kid raising hell, we want to blame the kid's parent. If you can blame the parent for the child's bad behavior, then maybe your child won't turn out like that wretched little demon, because you are not that parent. If the parent of that awful child is a complete jackass, then your kid will not turn out like that kid, because you are obviously not a complete jackass, right? Wrong. Sometimes, despite all that we do to be good parents, our kid turns out to be a complete jackass. What, that's not what you wanted to hear? Well, honestly, parenthood can be very discouraging, and one of the benefits of us not knowing each other is that I don't have to lie to you. Since the point of this chapter is to change your ideas about perfection, I am simply reminding you not to judge. This parenthood thing is hard. Hopefully, though, if we learn effective parenting techniques and apply them consistently, our personal little jackasses will eventually outgrow their jackassery. Hopefully.

CHAPTER SEVEN:

STOP TAKING THEIR CRAP SO PERSONALLY

STOP TAKING THEIR CRAP SO PERSONALLY

Now that you understand the the pitfalls of trying to be perfect, you need to stop taking everything your child says, does, wants, or needs personally. Please reread that last sentence, because it will change the way you parent. It is the key to successful parenting. It is the gold at the end of the rainbow.

We take everything so personally. We believe that their happiness is an ongoing referendum on our parenting ability. We have seen that having a well-behaved child does not make you a great mom. Having a naughty child does not make you a bad mom. Your child liking you does not make you a good parent. Your child disliking you does not make you a bad parent. When your child comes home at fifteen and tells you how cool Bubba's parents are because they let Bubba smoke pot as long as he does it with them, are you going to start your own neighborhood pot party? Of course not. That's because your job is to be his parent, not his best friend.

At some point, your wonderful little luvbug will declare his absolute hatred for you. Your three-year-old hates you because you won't give him any candy, your eleven-year-old hates you because you won't let her wear platform shoes, your seventeen-year-old hates you simply because he is seventeen. Listen people, your kids are going to hate you at some point. If this makes you a little nervous, I understand. You don't want your child to hate you. Well, calm down, because they don't really hate you. Your little heartbreaker is just mad. He is lashing out because you're not doing what he wants you to do. Being mad, disappointed, frustrated, or even sad when things don't go our way is normal and we all must learn how to deal with it.

I experienced a shift in this during my own youth. I moved in with my dad when I was about twelve. At my mom's place, I could not show any displeasure when I was in trouble. She would "slap that look off your face," ensuring that I would try to keep a neutral, blank expression whenever I was in trouble. I couldn't show any emotion, because then my punishment would be really bad. Thus I spent a lot of effort trying to look blank, rather than (quite reasonably) upset and a little scared. The first time I was in trouble with my dad, I reverted to my blank look. My dad stopped his tirade to ask me why I looked like such an idiot. After I explained the theory behind my blank look to him, my dad told me that my being unhappy with discipline is ok with him, as it was his desired result. So although he wouldn't tolerate disrespect, displeasure was certainly acceptable.

Think about it for a moment. Discipline should make your child feel discomfort. We reward them when they do the things we think are right. When we discipline them for the things we think are wrong, their unhappiness about it indicates that our methods are working. Stop taking it personally. We should tattoo this mantra on the insides of our eyelids. Remember, your child's not a slow learner. You're not a bad teacher. Remove your frustration by reminding yourself that your little gambler just placed another bet, and follow through with whatever discipline measures you have in place.

If your child declares how awful you are, how unfair it is, how your only goal in life is to make her miserable, you know you are on the right path. When your child declares their hatred for you, smile and thank them for letting you know you're doing a good job. This will accomplish two things: first, you will have removed any power from their statement. As we just established, your child is mad, so now he wants to say something that will make you feel just as bad as him. If you don't give him the desired result, his statement has no power. Second, you didn't get sucked into transference, which occurs when the actual issue gets sidelined because the encounter goes elsewhere. If your wounded little kitten bursts into tears and declares that you hate her, you might forget that she was caught smoking. Brilliant little goose, isn't she? But because you didn't take it personally, you didn't get caught up in transference. You smiled, pinched her little cheek and told her that she knows you don't hate her. Her smoking, on the other hand…

If you can stop taking it personally, then you can let go of any anger. You enabled these behaviors in your offspring by not using effective parenting techniques. It will take time and consistency for you to achieve the desired results, so sit back, take a deep breath, remind yourself that it isn't personal, and be as consistent and calm as possible. Eventually, you won't feel so frustrated, your child won't feel so frustrated, and your efforts will lead to a peaceful family environment.

CHAPTER EIGHT:

THE PITFALLS OF FAVORITISM

THE PITFALLS OF FAVORITISM

"How many times do I have to tell you?" you scream at your repeat offender. Taking it personally again? Stop it! Your little criminal isn't repeating the same behavior because he likes getting into trouble, or just to annoy you. He is repeating it because you're not being consistent, or because the discipline measures you are using are ineffective, perhaps even worth it to him. I could see my oldest child weighing the punishment against the crime. If I told him that if he ate any cookies before dinner he would have to stand in the corner, he would gladly stand in the corner. The corner was a fair price for the cookie, in his estimation. Not so for my daughter. If I required my girl to stand in the corner, she wouldn't eat the cookie. When my daughter was younger, we could not ground her to her room. Her room was her favorite place. The corner however, wasn't as pleasant for her. All of her imaginary friends lived in her room. She was happy there. However, my eldest hated being away from any action, so if I threatened to ground him to his room for eating a cookie, he wouldn't eat the cookie. If you find the right forms of discipline for your child, you will get the desired results.

This concept is invaluable to us as parents: find the right forms of discipline for your child to get the results you desire. Think about the personality of your child. My sweet little girl would die if she perceived that people were staring at her. This works wonderfully for me. I believe in complete disclosure with my kids, so I have outlined for them the consequences of all foreseeable bad actions. If my girl were caught stealing, she knows she could expect to stand in front of the store where the theft occurred, holding a sign declaring her crime to one and all. I have also reminded my children to consider that we live close to where we shop. Their friends live close to us, and probably shop close to where they live. Knowing what you do by now of my daughter, you can imagine how unworried I am about the chances she will shoplift.

Consider the personality of each individual child. One size does not fit all. If you have that obnoxious, stubborn, I-want-my-way-child, you must discipline her differently than the ready-to-please, nonconfrontational child. What may crush the sweet quiet child may not even affect the hell-on-wheels kid. When my daughter was a toddler, she would cry if I scolded her. She would even cry if I scolded her brother, which happened a lot. She doesn't like conflict. She wants the people around her to get along and be happy. She wants to do well and achieve approval. Her older brother was a completely different story. I could have been strangling him in the front yard and he wouldn't blink an eye. He doesn't care what other people think. Hell, he doesn't care what I think. He wants what he wants, when he wants it.

Here is where it gets tricky. Your little muffins cannot perceive any form of favoritism. Favoritism ruins sibling relationships. Do you want your children to grow up and be friends? Do you want them to be truly invested in each other's lives? If so, don't favor one or more of your children. I know that sometimes you like one more than the other, that maybe one sucks the joy right out of the day while the other is the light at the end of the tunnel. I know that you might understand one and not the other. Is it the easy one, the one that hugs you and tells you that you're the best? Or is it the other one, that naughty little thing? I know, because we all feel it. For me, it changes. I can feel really close to one and distant from the other, and then it will flip-flop. One makes me laugh more; one makes me think more. One is smarter, one is kinder, one is more interesting—and then they rotate. The one that I adored yesterday is making my world miserable today. Today he is pushing the limits.

You have probably figured out why this chapter follows the one on not taking it personally. Discipline is not personal. We need to modify it and apply it to the individual child, but because it is not personal, the standard of expected behavior does not change. The same rules apply to everyone. So, if talking back is not allowed in your house, then that must apply to everyone. Your most difficult child cannot get away with calling you a bitch just because she will kick and scream the whole time you're disciplining her, while your easiest gets his mouth washed out because he told you 'no'. Your punishments might vary based on the individual, but the rules on what is allowed must remain the same.

Children are very sensitive to fairness. The same rules must apply to everyone, with modifications for personalities and age. I think that parents having trouble with favoritism should sit down with all of their children and map out a list of transgressions. The transgressions are then followed by a list of the discipline measures that will result from that chosen activity. Laminate it and put it on the fridge. Then when the golden boy commits a felony on the list, he will know exactly what will happen. So will you. You will not be able to offer up any excuses for your golden boy. It will not matter that he was tired, bored, or just plain pissed off. If you always defer to the list, then you will not be able to show favoritism.

Your list can have different discipline measures for each child. Suppose that you, like us, have children of different age ranges. Let's use an eight-year-old, a fourteen-year-old, and a seventeen-year-old. Obviously, the eight-year-old and the seventeen-year-old will have different levels of discipline. For example, if the eight-year-old fails his spelling test, he is assigned more study time and less cartoons. If the seventeen-year-old flunks science, he loses his cell phone until he can show improvement. He definitely needs more study time, and the cell phone is too big of a distraction. It is vitally important for each child to know that the same rules apply to everyone; that all will be held to the same standards. The discipline is modified for age and personality, but the standard is always the same—in this case, that failing is unacceptable. Another example would be that if you smart mouth your mom, you will get into trouble, regardless of who you are, or why you did it.

I understand how detrimental favoritism is because I grew up in a household full of it. My older sister was awful. She was demanding, cruel, and manipulative. Never mind; she was adored and could do no wrong. It didn't matter to my mom what she did. I remember one time my sister came home drunk at age fourteen. I had been hiding in the hall because I knew something had happened; she was out way too late. When she finally came home and I realized she was drunk, I knew she was finally going to get in serious trouble. That didn't happen. She sat on the couch with my mom laughing and giggling, with the same woman who would have beaten me purple if I had done that. I realized at that moment that my mom would never love me the way she loved my sister. I hated my mom at that moment, but more disastrously, I also hated my sister. A sibling relationship likely to outlast my mother—and perhaps the relationship that might make all the difference for her in old age—was damaged at an impressionable age. Is there any parent that doesn't want his or her golden years comforted by loving children who love each other, enriched by grandchildren and great-grandchildren who hopefully stick together all their lives?

I understand now that my older sister would have done anything to maintain the position of being the favored child. However, that situation destroyed any chance that she would ever be close to my other sister or me. Children are supposed to be co-conspirators against their parents. They are supposed to commiserate about how awful you are and how other parents are better than theirs. My daughter recently told me about a time when I had separated my fighting children and sent them to their own rooms. Her older brother snuck into her room and gave her a walkie-talkie so they could talk about how unreasonable I was. She laughed while telling me this, feeling so proud because they got one over on me. In fact, I already knew about the walkie-talkies. I didn't intervene because it served my need for peace from their bickering and it warmed my heart. They banded together in that way that only siblings can. It was awesome.

Favoritism will rupture sibling relationships well into adulthood. My older sister is always absent from those fond memories my other sister and I share. We avoided her as children because she wouldn't hesitate to get us into trouble. In fact, in her eyes it was mandatory. In order to safeguard her position as the favored child, she had to sell us down the river. Her relationship with my mom had to be more important than the one she had with us. Knowing and feeling this, we didn't trust her. We didn't include her. We didn't confide in her. She was the enemy as far as we were concerned. Now, as adults, it is still that way.

Our kids go through phases. Phases pass. As parents, we also go through phases, and these also pass. Shifts in affection are just such phases. Since I know how much I love all of my children, simply for being my children, I can like one better today, I can like a different one better tomorrow. It really doesn't matter as long as I don't show favoritism—as long as I don't alter the standards. That would damage the relationships between our children, perhaps even destroy them forever.

CHAPTER NINE:

RESPECT

RESPECT

Parenting is a verb, people. Verbs convey action. Parenting requires action from us: effort, work. Where are your kids right now? Are they out front where you can see them? Are they down the block? Are they riding their bikes somewhere by the elementary school? Do you know who your kids are hanging out with? What are your kids doing at this minute? Note that the question is not "what do you think they are doing?" but "what are they doing?" It is your job to know what your kids are doing, where, and with whom. You think your little adventurers, at ten and eleven, are old enough to ride their bikes to the school to play on the big toys.

Maybe you didn't realize that they actually played basketball with the thirteen-year-old boys. Why is this a problem? It's a problem if you don't know those boys. For all you know, they've been sneaking off to smoke pot since they were twelve. Perhaps your little guy thinks they are super cool. The little potheads get this admiration by default, simply because they are older. What kind of influence will these future convicts have over your impressionable wee ones? Who the hell knows? You certainly don't, because you didn't even know they were hanging out with your kid!

I realize that, for the majority of parents, it is much easier to let your child go play and just ask them when they return what they did. Of course, because children are perfect little people, they would never tell you that the neighbor caught them going through his garage. They neglected to mention that after one mom told them that her kids couldn't play, they continued to knock on all the windows and doors, until the same mom informed them that they should go home and annoy their own mom with this fun activity. Oh, did they forget to mention that they banded together, the way unattended children do, to pick on the little guy that doesn't play basketball as well as they do?

Time to get off the couch, hang up the phone, and pay your kids as much attention as you give Facebook. Find out what they are doing, who they are playing with, who they are talking to, and how they are playing with others. As parents, we need to take advantage of these opportunities to do some parenting. When they grow into teenagers, they will no longer listen to your guidance. The opportunity to redirect their thinking will have passed. It is crucial to know what your kids are doing, who they are playing with, and what influences they have.

Let's use our inept little basketball player from above: if one of those parents had known how badly those children were treating the unathletic little player, they could have taken that moment to teach their little bully some empathy. What if the parents had stopped the game and explained to the hotshots that, although they imagined themselves NBA pros, their mistreatment of a less capable player in fact made them losers? What if they had told them how disappointed this made them, as parents? The opportunity to teach something profound didn't happen for those parents. The majority of the time, they had no idea what their kids were actually doing.

If that humiliated, disheartened little player had been mine, I would have taken that opportunity to teach him that not everyone else is considerate of others and their abilities. While it sucks to be the kid that can't do something as well as everyone else, it sucks far worse to be the kid who is mean to someone else simply because they can't do something. I'd point out that the other boys' moms probably did not respect their sons, and were probably not proud of them—I certainly wouldn't be. I'd tell my son that I hoped he realized that those kids are not the kind of kids he wants as friends. Why be friends with people you can't be proud of? If we don't know what our kids are doing, we miss many teaching moments. We never get them back.

One of the parents in my neighborhood believes that because she doesn't allow her boys to go into other people's backyards, they are fine. What? Seriously? In fact, it explains a lot. When these boys, who are in the second and third grade, were walking to school one day, I watched them beat the crap out of another neighbor's fence with large sticks. Unless the fence owner informs this mom of her boys' activities, she will have no idea that her boys are destroying someone's property. I doubt that the boys ran home and told their parents how much fun it was destroying someone else's fence. But this mom isn't worried. They were not in the backyard, after all.

This mentality leads to all sorts of bad things. We have to know what our children are doing. I don't understand why we waste our time teaching our children to say 'please' and 'thank you' if we don't bother to teach them respect for other people and their property. Perhaps some parents think their child is so important he should be able to ride your kid's Big Wheel without permission; 'they are just kids, after all.' They shouldn't act shocked when those same kids get arrested in their teens for stealing or vandalism. Think it'll never happen to your kid? Okay. When do you think they learn that they can't do what they want, when they want? Do you think that lesson happens when they turn sixteen? Nope, it happens when they are three. It happens when they are seven. It happens when you say, "Get out of there, that is not your yard," "Put that back, you didn't ask them to use it," or "Play ball in the field because you don't want to hit someone's car." Of course, to do this, you must know what your child is doing.

As a parent, I believe I must teach my children respect for other people's property. If our ball flies into your backyard, my kids aren't permitted to just jump your fence and retrieve the wayward ball. They will knock on your front door, explain the situation, and ask permission to retrieve the ball. I recently watched the neighborhood children hook up a water slide in one neighbor's front lawn and have a happy slip-n-slide party. There was only problem: the residential neighbor's household was not part of the party. Imagine my pride to note that not only were my kids not out enjoying the brand new water park, but that they were shocked. This was the result of a lot of parenting: checking on them, listening to dialogue between them and their peers, intervening as needed, and redirecting them if they go somewhere they have no business. My hope is to avoid picking them up from the police station after their arrests for vandalism.

Here's a good rule for kids to grasp: if it wasn't yours to begin with, it's not yours now. In other words, if it was not yours when we came here, you aren't taking it with you. If you have taught your child to respect others' property, this lesson is not far behind. We all have that moment when we find something neat and want to keep it. When my oldest was in grade school, he found a baseball bat. He was so excited because he thought he was going to keep it. Not so, wee one. I asked him how sad he thought the boy who lost his bat would be when he returned to get it, and it was gone? After deciding that the boy would indeed be sad, we then decided it wouldn't be right to take the bat with us. This rule applies to everything. That same boy of mine once found a pretty little Black

Hills gold ring in a restaurant. I really, really liked that ring. But I am a parent above all; the boy will follow my example. It didn't belong to us, sadly, so we turned it in to the manager. As it turned out, an elderly couple had lost the ring, so he actually got to see the couple's joy at the return of their lost treasure. More importantly for him, he got to see the right example from his mom.

The lessons we teach our young children lead and build into the bigger lessons later in life. The only way to teach them to respect people and property is to pay attention and actively parent your children.

CHAPTER TEN:

UNGRATEFULNESS GETS YOU NOTHING

UNGRATEFULNESS GETS YOU NOTHING

Several years ago, I was celebrating the Christmas holiday with one of my sisters-in-law and her family. On Christmas morning, after opening her last gift, one of my darling nieces threw herself on the floor, kicking and screaming. She threw her other presents. She screamed horrible things at her parents. Finally, after her tirade was over, she curled up in the fetal position. It turns out that her heart's desire was a laptop. Much to her shock and dismay, her parents couldn't afford a laptop. I have never before or since witnessed such a lack of gratitude in another human being. Needless to say, I never spent another Christmas morning at my sister-in-law's house.

That experience had a profound impact on how I feel about gratitude, and in turn on my parenting emphasis. My little elves will display fervent gratitude for the slippers their grandma knitted them with her mismatched yarn. They will benevolently praise your efforts to please their taste with your chosen confection. If my daughter receives the same Barbie she already owns, she will gladly proclaim that she now has twins. My children have come to understand that ungratefulness gets you nothing.

It starts when they are the littlest of people. Unless the size is wrong, or there is a defect, we do not let them return presents. I decided not to allow them to trade gifts in for gift cards to get what they really wanted. If our kids really want something, they can learn to work for it, save their own money, and buy it themselves. A gift is something that someone wanted the child to have, put time and thought into, and deserves the child's appreciation for that. Perfect or not, what he wanted or not, it was still something special for the child. Someone cared enough about him to get it. And that is why I expect mine to show gratitude. Always. If they do not, they will get nothing.

Gratitude and expectation is a tree with many branches for parents to cover. My children won't send you a list of their birthday or Christmas demands. At best, people can ask me, since I'm their mom and I know what they would really like. Otherwise they get what they get. We raised them not to expect anything, that holidays are not obligations. Let's consider people who don't celebrate holidays and birthdays. Our children need to learn that it doesn't mean that those people don't love you, just that they don't celebrate. Some people are on very fixed incomes. What if your child gave them a list of his fondest birthday desires and they couldn't afford anything? Ask him if he would really want a present from his great grandpa if it meant Gramps had to go without his frozen turkey dinner?

When my children display ingratitude, they receive nothing. When my boy was about seven, we went to a store where they gave free cookies to cute little boys. He informed our free cookie hostess that he didn't want one of her free cookies; he wanted something else. "That was not what you were offered," I responded sadly. "Your ungratefulness gets you nothing." The bakery attendant gave me a horrible look, for which I could pardon her.

To her, it seemed I was being overly strict, and should have given my sorrowful little guy another chance. I saw an opportunity to teach him about the importance of gratitude, without my sad little cookie monster losing too much. Later, I reminded him to be grateful for what he is offered, and to be glad it was only a cookie that he went without.

This principle applies to everything. At the fantastic age of fourteen, my other son informed me that the dinner I made was crap. Aren't kids fun? Well, I'm certainly no gourmet, but my dinners are edible. After all, they have sustained him his whole life. So, I calmly took away his plate and scraped it into the garbage, while explaining that he didn't have to eat it. Of course, he wasn't getting anything else. Ungratefulness gets you nothing.

I know that a grateful attitude will bring them joy in the future. If people feel no pressure to get you the perfect gift, or spend such and such an amount of money, it's rather fun to see what people will get you.

CHAPTER ELEVEN:

TIMEOUT CAN HAPPEN ANYWHERE

TIMEOUT CAN HAPPEN ANYWHERE

Do you remember when your little three-year-old cherub was naughty, and you put his cute, chubby little butt in the timeout spot? It got to the point where all you had to say was, "Do you want a timeout?" You can adapt it to your older children as well; it is a tried-and-true method with a lot of power, provided you evolve it with their ages. I was arguing with my nine-year-old at the fair one year. It really sucks to have to discipline at the fair. What can you do? You're not going to go home, although you probably threatened it. My little clown thought he had it all figured out. We were over by the barns and I had finally had it. I was done warning and threatening him. So I walked him over to the outside of the barn wall and required him to put his nose on the wall. If you have ever been to the livestock section of a fair, you have an idea of the fragrance. Visualize standing in the corner, but with the smell of cows and pigs surrounding you. I reminded him that the fair was a very busy place, but not to worry; if I saw any of his friends, I would wave and yell that he was presently in time out. I also reminded him that when he could behave appropriately, he could say hi to them too.

How long should a timeout be? I have no time requirement on timeouts. It is a popular concept to keep your child in time out for a number of minutes equal to his or her age. I think this is a great place to start, but I wonder how effective it is for the stubborn, strong willed child. If, after being removed from the timeout, your child continues the misbehavior, how effective was the timeout?

Not knowing can be worse than any set amount of time. I have found this to be a great deterrent. To decide when timeout will end, I consider two factors, the first of which is whether I'm done being angry. It doesn't end until I cool down. Here's an illustration: while waiting in line to pick up my young son and his friend from school, I observed them picking on another child in line. When we returned to my home, I put both boys—yes, including the friend—in timeout. The friend asked my son how many minutes time out lasted in our house. My son sadly informed him that there wasn't any time limit, and because I was pretty mad at their behavior, they might be in time out for a while.

The second factor requires the child to convince me that he or she won't repeat the behavior that earned a timeout. My kids have learned, to their pain, that I can be very hard to convince. This requires serious dialogue about the transgression. It would be so easy to simply do six minutes of time out and then let your child run off to play, but does that give any assurance that your little fluff ball understands what she did? That is the purpose, to assure that she understands and will not repeat the behavior again. I don't care if it takes two minutes or twenty minutes. I don't want my child to watch the clock obsessively waiting for the allotted time to run out. I want her thinking that whatever she did wasn't worth this unpleasantness.

Here's another example of timeout use at a later age, I was grocery shopping, which I hate, because it always feels like I am giving away my money. Everything I buy is going to be eaten. I won't have a cool new pair of jeans that shapes and lifts my backside to perfection. I won't have sparkly new earrings to enjoy. Worse yet, I'll have to turn around and do it again in a week. And now I have to do something with all this food, probably involving cooking, which I don't enjoy. I only do it because my family whines about how hungry they are. During one particularly tortuous shopping experience, my thirteen-year-old decided that this was a great time to argue about what cereal he wanted. I was not a model of empathy. I explained that he didn't live alone in a little box; as a family of five, we had to choose cereal everyone would eat. Do you think that my little speech curbed his attitude? Do you imagine he let up on his struggle for his favorite cereal? Do you suppose he took into consideration how much I hate grocery shopping? If you do, today is not your day to buy a lottery ticket.

Remember criss-cross-applesauce? You probably did it in kindergarten when your teacher wanted you all to sit on the floor. She said, "criss-cross-applesauce," and you all sat on the floor with your legs crossed in front of you and your hands clasped in your laps. That is my solution to the grocery shopping argument: timeout in the grocery store. While he sat on the floor, legs crossed, hands clasped in his lap, I calmly looked at the cereal. I weighed the importance of price vs. flavor, and explained to anyone who passed by us to ignore him because he was in time out. Grocery shopping is very peaceful for me now.

Do your children know that time out can happen anywhere, or do they think since you're at the store, the fair, the doctor's office, the school, they have all the power? Which understanding do you think is likely to lead to a higher public behavior standard?

CHAPTER TWELVE:

LOSER LOSER

LOSER LOSER

"This game sucks!" your little butterball complains as he crosses his arms and stomps out of the room. We have all had that moment, haven't we? Your precious little person isn't winning, and is therefore having a miserable time. Now what do you do?

Well, you could coddle your little loser and try to coax him back into the game. You could make a few bad moves yourself and throw the game so he comes from behind to (crowd cheers in background) win the game! What a victory! The comeback kid resurrects his loss and turns it around to a win! Oh, wait, he didn't come back to beat the odds. He didn't strategize and play smarter. He didn't dig down deep and work all that much harder. In fact, he didn't win at all. If you handled it that way, you cheated. Actually, you didn't just cheat at the game; you also cheated your child.

We don't always get to win. Losing is part of life. You can't win everything, every time. Learning how to lose is an invaluable lesson for children. It teaches a multitude of things: to work harder, study more, triumph over obstacles, and have empathy for others. Be assured that your child's peers will not be so understanding of her poor loser attitude. Her future coach will not be tolerant of her tantrum on the field. Her tears won't get her one more shot to impress her bosses.

How do we teach our children to lose? We play games with them. We don't cheat and we don't allow them to cheat. When my children tried to cheat, I would calmly get up and leave the game, stating that I don't play with cheaters. I then explained that I would rather lose honestly and have fun simply playing the game then win dishonestly. When they start down the road to Losers' Lane with comments and attitudes, I pull them back and remind them that the loser behavior will not be tolerated. Show your child sportsmanship by your own conduct when you lose. Teach them that the more you play, the better you get. You need to acknowledge their smart strategic moves. You need to high-five their successes, even when they're losing, commending them on how well they played.

If they persist in bad attitudes and rude comments, they should be removed from the game while everyone else enjoys the family fun. Poor losers can't be tolerated. Rude behavior and comments should mean immediate removal from the game. "I didn't want to play anyway," they will scathe at you. "Good," you can reply, "because your attitude is unacceptable. However, when you decide to play nicely, you can rejoin the game." When the game is over, whether your child rejoined or not, you can pat him on the head and say, "That was a fun game, maybe next time you can play the whole thing."

When my daughter was fourteen, she received an invitation to participate in a fashion event. She was so excited. The girls showed their gowns by gracefully posing across the stage. Big, beautiful smiles, accessories galore; they looked so beautiful, each and every one. Yet, at the awards ceremony, when there was only one winner, there was an abundance of tears and sadness. Several of these beautiful girls, who minutes before had pranced across the stage displaying their beauty with pride, were now crying because they didn't win. My preciousness was beaming. As I hugged her and told her how proud we were of her, I asked her if she was disappointed. She explained that although winning would have been most excellent, she hadn't really expected to win. This was her first event, after all. She really had no idea what to expect, what to do, or what exactly the judges were looking for. She felt that it had been an amazing time; she had made some awesome new friends, she felt incredibly beautiful up there, and in general had loved the experience. When your child handles it this way, as a parent, you get a double dose of pride. You're proud of how she participated, and even more proud of her poised attitude toward the result.

Maybe if we focus on the playing, instead of the winning, we can help our children understand the importance of trying new things and enjoying their individual successes. We can help them see that losing is just an indication of what you need to learn. We can help them set goals, practice, follow through, and work harder. We can give them the tools to be successful, so they can experience the awards that come with something well deserved and well earned.

CHAPTER THIRTEEN:

LESSONS IN BOREDOM

LESSONS IN BOREDOM

My friend brought his child over to play. While the kids played, my friend told me how upset he was about his son. His adorable boy was acting out in class. His child would randomly get up and walk around, fidgeting and distracting others. When he asked the child why he was misbehaving, he said that he was bored. "Oh, that's easily remedied," I explained to his father. "You can have lessons in boredom." Yeah, that's right, you can teach your child how to be bored. And honestly, you probably should. As grownups, we know that life isn't always fun and games. Actually, it's often rather boring. But our pre-computer childhood prepared us for this. Our parents told us to go outside and play. We had to entertain ourselves. We had to learn to wait for things. We sat in the cart while our parents grocery shopped, and we didn't have the entertainment of a Nintendo DS.

Our kids have a disadvantage in this area, growing up in the computer technology generation. They are not expected to use their imaginations or entertain themselves. There are super cool game systems that will do it for them. We now have DVD players on the backs of the headrests in our cars. Our kids do not have to look out the window when driving to the corner store; they can watch a movie. Does this all seem a little ridiculous to you? No wonder children have trouble being bored, when they grow up with the expectation of constant entertainment.

When my kids came to me complaining that they were bored, I would explain to them that I didn't consider it my job to entertain them constantly. However, if they needed something to do, I could arrange that: I would assign them a cleaning job. My children were not 'bored' very often. They learned how to entertain themselves, not expect someone else to do it for them.

As my friend's child was discovering, school isn't always going to be fun. Sometimes it's about learning. Sometimes it's boring. This brings us to the lessons in boredom. If your child's behavior mimics my friend's little guy, you can have your bored little bunny sit in a chair, in the middle of the kitchen, with nothing to do for a lengthy period of time. Don't allow her to talk or get up. Have her sit and…wait. That's it. Just wait. After her time is up, remind her that if she cannot behave during class time tomorrow, you can practice again. And again...and again, if necessary. It's up to them.

This lesson starts at home, but transfers to other areas. Our children need to learn the life lesson that they are not the most important people in the room. Sometimes, someone else needs to be the center of attention. Sometimes someone else is more important than they are. Sometimes, you just have to wait. We all sometimes have to wait: doctor's office, emergency room, even the Land of Mordor where the shadows lie (better known as the DMV). Teach your kids that they must sit quietly in their seats and do what is expected of them at school. Teach your children that when they're done with their assignments, they must wait patiently for the next thing to happen; that they are not allowed to interrupt their teachers or their classmates by being disruptive. Your child's teacher will thank you.

Of course, common sense must apply. There is boredom, and there is ADD or ADHD. If you are concerned about hyperactivity or any other childhood disorders, please take your child for a medical evaluation. I advise you to talk to your doctor about your concerns and your child's behavior. Under their supervision I propose trying the methods outlined in this book for thirty days. The first week will be very difficult because your child may rebel against your new found concepts. However, with consistency your child's behavior should gradually improve. If despite a diligent good faith effort over the thirty day period, you still feel like your child needs medication, then at least you know you did everything possible before exercising that option.

CHAPTER FOURTEEN:

NOSES TOUCHING

NOSES TOUCHING

Do your children bicker constantly? Mine used to. They would bicker about anything and everything, from whose turn it was to clean the bathroom to which of them the dog loved more. It did not matter what it was, my children would fight about it. Not anymore. I finally put an end to it.

I was standing in the kitchen after a long day at work, trying to come up with something imaginative for dinner. Although I was doing my best to tune them out, there they were in the kitchen with me, fighting. I do not know where this came from, but I said the next thing that popped into my head. "Stand with your noses touching!"

Have you ever had a brilliant idea, one that shocks you with sudden recognition of its power? This was such a moment. I was tingly from my head to my toes. I had thought of something so powerful right then and I knew it. My kids knew it too. I could tell because shock and fear registered on their precious little faces. "What? No way!" they cried. "Yep," I said. "Noses touching. NOW!"

Take a few minutes and picture this. Every time your children bicker, you have them stop and put their noses together. It is perfect. Children do not like to touch their siblings, except to inflict pain on them. Here they are, standing face to face, hands behind their backs, with their noses touching. At first they will verbally revolt, "I am not doing that!" Respond calmly: "Yes, you are. You were arguing." Them: "This is stupid." Your reply: "So is your fighting." After a moment of their noses touching, one of them will probably crack a smile, and then the other one will smile. Then one of them will laugh, and then the other one will laugh. At that point the exercise is over. The fight will have lost its importance.

This exercise has so much power because the threat of having to stand with their noses physically touching has a great impact on their behavior. When my children start bickering, all I have to do is touch my nose and smile. As an added bonus, it is hilarious to watch.

This works very well for grade school children. It is awesome for middle-schoolers. By high school, the mere threat of it is all you need. Does it work on toddlers? Probably not. Toddlers are learning about self-control and how they fit in their universe. They do not yet have goals like torturing their siblings. They are not fighting just for the sake of fighting.

CHAPTER FIFTEEN:

THE ART OF SENTENCE WRITING

THE ART OF
WRITING SENTENCES

I love sentences. I cannot emphasize enough how effective sentence writing can be. How did I get my children to scrape the food off their dishes before loading them into the dishwasher? One little person in my house had to write: "Contrary to what I would like to think, there is no little man in the dishwasher who scrapes and scrubs the crud off the dishes. Therefore, it is necessary for me to scrape and rinse my own dishes before loading them."

How did I decrease any name calling among my offspring? If they take part in name calling, I have them write: "I will not call my little brother names. It is rude and unnecessary to express my displeasure this way. Besides, I love my little brother. He is a great brother and I am so lucky to have him."

If they go in each other's rooms without permission, I have had them write: "It is not ok for me to be in my sister's room when she is gone. It is an invasion of her privacy, and only my Mom and Dad can invade her privacy, since they pay the mortgage and I don't."

If one of my little people is disrespectful to an educator, he has to write: "My teacher went to school for many years to impart her knowledge to me. It would be very tough to teach a bunch of ungrateful teenagers and yet she gets up every day to bless us with her knowledge. I apologize for my disrespect." He then must take the completed sentences to the offended teacher, have the teacher sign it, and then return it to me. You will probably only have to do that once. It is rather embarrassing for the school-aged smart-ass.

One parent I know has their child write definitions directly out of the dictionary. This is a double dose of parental genius, educational and effective. For example, if her child is insensitive to a family member she writes: Insensitive - thoughtless, indifferent to the importance of something, insufficiently aware of other people's feelings and unable to respond to them appropriately, not responsive to a physical stimulus such as touch or sound.

I think that parents don't use sentence writing because it can be very hard to enforce. My sister called me on the phone to lament that her daughter was rebelling against writing sentences. After crying and begging for a different punishment, my darling niece crossed her arms and declared that she simply wasn't going to write the sentences. After reinforcing for my sis that her daughter's reaction showed that the sentences were absolutely the right discipline choice, I suggested that it wasn't an option to debate that with her precious love.

I advised her to explain to her child that nothing, and I mean nothing, happens until the sentences are done. She sits at the table, away from any television or distractions, until the sentences are completed. She does not talk to siblings or friends. She does not receive phone calls. She does not text. She does not watch television. She does not pet the puppy or cuddle the cat. She is to sit at the designated spot until the sentences are completed. If mealtime approaches and she has not completed the task, then she can resume her writing activity when mealtime is over. If bedtime arrives, she can resume the writing activity the next day. I don't care if it takes her twenty minutes or two days, nothing happens until the sentences are completed. Initially this will be difficult for you and your child, but stay firm, calm, and patient. This is one of the best wrenches in the parental tool belt. Follow through with this technique once, and the mere threat of sentencing your little felon to sentences will accomplish more than you can imagine.

CHAPTER SIXTEEN:

TAKE ALL THE TIME YOU NEED

TAKE ALL THE TIME YOU NEED

"Take all the time you need."

That's all I have to say, and my children will scramble. I am a freak about time. I hate being late, because I think it tells people that your time is more important than theirs. I don't mind the occasional lateness, but habitual lateness really bothers me.

Every parent knows how easy it is to end up habitually late. Two or more kids make it almost impossible to be on time for anything. Sometimes it is an amazing feat to get out of the house at all. The amount of baggage that children require is enough to frustrate the most patient person. Throw in the teenager whose hair isn't combed, the girl who can't find anything to wear, the kid who can't find his backpack, or the one who informs you that he forgot to eat breakfast, and think creatively about the possibilities for delay.

Well, I got tired of it. I hate being late. Furthermore, I hate freaking out every morning over the same silly issues: Turn off the TV and get ready. What do you mean you didn't brush your teeth yet? You had shoes yesterday, so logic would indicate that they must be here somewhere! I don't care what level you are on, stop playing your video game, and get in the car! You have to poop *now*?

Because my children are old enough to understand that they need to be ready at certain times, and because I want them to understand that late equals rude, I needed to come up with a way to pound the message home. I decided to make them repay me the time that they wasted.

Here is how it works:

Mom: "It's time to go."

Child: "I can't find my [your choice of item]."

Mom: "It is 8:40. Take all the time you need."

From 8:40 on, I keep track of the time. When the child is ready, I inform him of the time deficit he has created. If it took him seven minutes to be ready, he owes me seven minutes of my chosen activity, which can be anything that amuses me. It could be seven minutes of jumping jacks. Maybe the floor really needs to be vacuumed. Perhaps my aching feet will need a massage. It might even suit my whim to hear one of them sing,

'I'm a Little Teapot.' That one is very effective for your teenage boy.

Yes, you will still be late, but only the first few times. Remember what we discussed about the importance of consistency. If you are consistent, it will not take very long for the little tardy turtles to catch on and improve their time management greatly.

This is also really effective at bedtime, especially if you use the owed time by waking them up extra early, so they can make you toast.

CHAPTER SEVENTEEN:

YOU TEACH PEOPLE HOW TO TREAT YOUR SIBLING

YOU TEACH PEOPLE HOW TO TREAT YOUR SIBLING

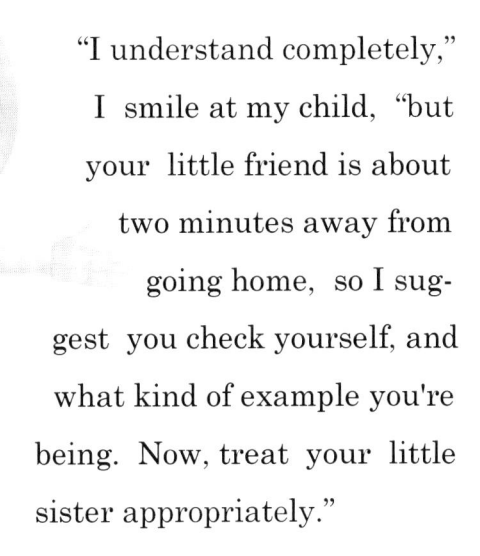

"I understand completely," I smile at my child, "but your little friend is about two minutes away from going home, so I suggest you check yourself, and what kind of example you're being. Now, treat your little sister appropriately."

Siblings are annoying. I get that. When your kid has his friend over, they want that precious new person all to themselves. Everything the precious new person does is interesting and profound. Everybody wants to be with the precious new person, who is not one of the same old boring people, who reside in the same old boring house, every same old boring day. 'Everybody' includes your child's siblings. She wants nothing more than to bask in the glow of the sibling's new friend. Now, that presents a problem, doesn't it?

Your child doesn't want to share his new friend with anyone in your house. Your child wants to play fun games, with only his friend. Your child wants to be alone with his friend while they listen to music or watch movies. Your child wants to have long, interesting, profound conversations with his friend. He wants to seem cool to this friend, for him to have so much fun at your house that he will want to come back.

So, what do you do as the parent? You can understand both viewpoints, especially if you were ever a child with a sibling. The lazy parent's way is to make a hard and fast rule that no one can have any friends over. That sounded great to me, but my children rebelled at the concept. I had to teach my children that they teach people how to treat their siblings.

If your child calls her sibling names while their friend is present, the friend will call the sibling names. If your child complains to her friend how stupid her sibling is, then their friend will come to agree. If your child is rude, impatient, selfish, or just plain ugly to her sibling, then you can expect her friend to follow suit. It isn't the friend's fault. She is just following your kid's example. The friend doesn't want to go home. She likes your house. Her house is boring. It has the same old boring people, every same old boring day, doing the same old boring things. She wants to come back to your house. She thinks your kid is cool, and wants your kid to think she's cool. Because she wants your kid to like her, she follows your child's example.

Let's ponder one more concept before we talk about how to balance this situation. Our home should be where we always feel the safest, and have peace and acceptance, right with our families. Your children leave every day and are knocked around by the world. Growing up is hard. Children are mean. Teachers aren't always kind. Friends aren't always friends. Your children need a soft place to fall, probably more than you do. Your children do not need, nor do they deserve, to be tortured by their siblings' friends in their own homes.

So, how do you balance this? Have you ever had your own friend over? Then you understand that your children will do the same exact thing to you and your friend. My kids will all gather around when my friends are over, hanging on every word we say. This completely amazes me, because we are boring as hell. We are grown ups. We don't want to curl each other's hair and listen to music. We talk about dull crap like bills, what to make for dinner, or the $400 visit to the veterinarian. But my kids think my friend is new and interesting, so I let them visit with us. I let them hang out for a while. Then I politely send them on their way, explaining that we want some alone time.

That's what you do with your kids and their friends. You have them acknowledge their siblings. You remind them that their siblings are little people, with feelings, and it's hard to be the one left out. You encourage them to let their siblings be involved if possible. Obviously your daughter's little sister can't help big sister and her friend with their homework, but she can watch cartoons with them. You then encourage the left out siblings to give them some alone time. You explain to the left out child that when she has a friend over, she will want some alone time too. Next, you find something amazing and fun for the poor left out child to do. You could bake cookies, play a game, or watch a movie. You could even have your adult friend back over, so your left out little gal can follow the two of you around.

What you don't do is waver from the expectation. If your child and their friend do not treat the sibling with kindness, the friend goes home. If the friend is kind, but your child treats their sibling unkindly, the friend goes home. Your child sets the example. This principle is nonnegotiable. I think it's a very bad idea to tolerate anyone coming into your home, then treating anyone in your family unkindly. It's also a bad situation if the arrival of someone else in your home ruptures the home's peace and safety for anyone who lives there. It might not be the friend's fault, but taking him home is how you teach your child. You will only have to take one friend home, one time, to see dramatic results from your children.

CHAPTER EIGHTEEN:

TRASH TALKING AND TENACITY

TRASH TALKING AND TENACITY

Parenthood requires tenacity. If we are to prevail as parents we must first lay out our rules, expectations, and discipline measures. Then, if our children fail to live up to our stated expectations, and they might, we must follow through with the promised consequences. Finally, we must firmly commit to make our child's life hell until the consequences are completed. We must be tenacious in this. At some point your delinquent teenager will finally submit to the consequences, proclaiming that he or she is only doing it because it is easier than fighting you. Let's consider that. Teenagers will eventually oblige us, the parents, because it is easier than arguing. The child does what the parent wants, because it is easier than fighting the parents. How many times have you heard the opposite story? Isn't it usually the parents that are exhausted fighting the teenagers?

Somewhere along the line, most of us probably imagined that our kids would reach those preteen/teen years, and parenting wouldn't be such hard work. Not so. Teenagers are work. They are faced with serious, life-altering situations every day. They are full of hormones and battered by peer pressure. It is crucially important that you are an active parental force in your child's life throughout the teenage years. This is not the time to claim exhaustion. You can't allow yourself the option of giving up, no matter how tired you are.

Remember how important being consistent was in the toddler years and apply those same concepts now. Remind yourself that being consistent is essential in helping you change behaviors, and how integral it is in achieving a peaceful family environment. When we are consistent our children learn that we mean what we say and therefore they will fight us less over the consequences. In fact, the more consistent and persistent we are, the less they will challenge us and break the rules.

This brings us to the real life example: my son was arguing with me yet again. I construed this as disrespect. I labeled this trash talking and informed my indignant boy that he would now be participating in a roadside trash collecting field trip. This would give him time to contemplate the insolent rubbish he had said to his lovely Mom. My husband brought home a bright orange vest from work so our son would be safe while collecting trash. "How in the world did you get him to do that?" my son's aunt asked me. "He knows I will make his life miserable until it's done," I replied.

How do you get a 6'2" bruiser to put on a vest and pick up trash? You give him a choice. I explained to him that, although he continued to be disrespectful even after being warned, he had options. I went on about what a patient, merciful, fair parent I was, which meant that if he picked up the trash without any grief, I would let him select the location of our trash collecting field trip. However, if he continued to fight me (because he was definitely going on our trash collecting trip and nothing was going to happen in his life until it was completed), I would pick the location. I was envisioning the rather filthy area in front of his high school. Needless to say, he jumped out of bed and asked where the vest was.

My son, being the smart ass that he is, picked the most obscure location he could find. We traveled up this winding country road until I finally said 'enough.' I parked the car, gave him a black garbage bag and settled in for an amusing afternoon. Two minutes later, my son returned to our car with an abandoned car door and explained that it wouldn't fit in the garbage bag, but he was trying to be thorough. Having a smart, funny kid can be such a pain in the ass.

I imagine having a smart, funny, tenacious mom can also be a pain in the ass.

CHAPTER NINETEEN:

MOMMY WORDS AND TEA PARTIES

MOMMY WORDS
AND TEA PARTIES

Yes, I cuss frequently. I love the way the word 'fuck' feels when I say it. I like the word 'bitch,' which represents strength and confidence to me. It reminds me not to take people's crap. My children have often heard me mumble 'jackass' when someone cuts me off in traffic. It makes me feel better. I have a picture that my littlest drew for me in second grade. I am a stick figure with a blue head. The caption he wrote above it says, "you ass." That is my favorite picture.

However, my children do not cuss. I have taught them that those are "mommy/daddy words." They are not allowed to use them, on penalty of a spoonful of vinegar. It is no more hypocritical of me than allowing myself alcohol (another adult privilege), while denying them. Children don't understand that certain words alienate certain people, which an adult should. I recognize that some groups wouldn't welcome me because of my language, for example, and an adult can decide to be okay with that. Swearing also protects me from invitations to church events and Tupperware parties, neither of which interest me.

Children also do not grasp that there are times not to cuss at all, whereas an adult does (or should). A child who is allowed to swear might end up swearing during your grandfather's funeral, which is pretty disrespectful. Teenagers don't take such matters into account, and many don't understand how offensive certain language can be to certain groups or in certain situations. They don't realize how it could affect them or someone else. They just think that they are cool. So, in my house and for my family, only adults get to use bad language. It is a privilege of adulthood, much like getting to drink a cold beer at the end of a hot summer day because you're over twenty-one.

Just because I cuss in front of my children, however, doesn't mean I cuss at them. I don't do it, ever, nor do I believe any parent should. There are parents who call their daughter a bitch, a slut, a whore, which I find both appalling and abusive. It follows that I consider it disastrously bad parenting, damaging to your child's soul. In fact, my rule for myself is never to call my children names at all. When their parents call them lazy, stupid, fat or whatever, it's destructive.

It is not good enough to let it slip, then come back later and give them some shit about how you didn't mean it and were just 'so mad.' Abusing a child this way demonstrates an unforgivable lack of self-control on your part—the exact thing you worked so hard to teach them. It will also cost you their respect.

We also do not allow name calling in our home. Not me, their dad, their siblings, their grandpa, grandma, aunts, uncles, or anyone. Ever. Words have a huge impact on us. They stay with us, impairing self-esteem for years. The names you call your children, (this would include any swear words) or allow others to call them, they will probably learn to accept deep down, meaning that someday in the future they'll accept the same verbal abuse from other people. Put another way: would you want to bear responsibility for your daughter spending her life with some jackass who constantly tells her (just like Dad did) how stupid and useless she is? Do you want your gems to believe in their hearts that they are worthless? Are you prepared for the day that they come back and tell you how horrible you made them feel? You, the one person who was supposed to love them?

I hope we are perfectly clear on this issue. I don't get invited to a lot of genteel, hats-and-gloves, extended-pinky-finger garden tea parties. I may be an improper, cuss-like-you-mean-it, sassy bitch, but my little cupcakes think that they are the frosting that makes everything yummy. And yours should think that too.

CHAPTER TWENTY:

SNEAKING OUT

SNEAKING OUT

One night my friend's thirteen-year-old daughter snuck out to meet a boy she met on the Internet. Are you horrified? My friend was, as was I when she told me about it. Even my daughter was horrified. This is the perfect example of how stupid teenagers can be. We as adults know how dangerous this is. I bet your stomach becomes nauseous just thinking about your son or daughter doing something so stupid.

This is why it is so important for us to maintain a continuous dialogue with our kids. We need to point out every example we can find of risky behaviors. If your child is old enough to have an email or a Facebook page, you must educate him or her about how predators victimize kids: how they find and groom victims, tactics of luring them to the meeting, and what happens then. Fortunately, TV is full of shows about this. Have them watch with you, so they can see that it may not be a fourteen-year-old soccer player they are chatting with, but a forty-eight-year-old pervert. Make them watch the news program of the teenager kidnapped from her home. Make them read the newspaper articles. If they know how the bad guys work, they can recognize it when they see it starting. Make them understand that if adults get kidnapped, raped, and murdered every day, then so can the super smart, careful, invincible teenager.

After you have educated them about the evils in the world, you need to be very clear on the consequences if they fail to follow the rules you have in place. For example: "If you sneak out, not only will you lose all computer rights and privacy, you will have new roommates. You will share a room with your Dad and I. We will put a twin mattress on our floor for your bed, and you will sleep in our room. We will sing a good night song to you, and pat you on the head before bed. We will remind you that your safety is our utmost concern. When your friends come over, we will make sure they get the tour, so we can show them your new sleeping arrangements." You probably understand why my daughter was horrified.

CHAPTER TWENTY-ONE:

BULLIES

BULLIES

Schools are taking bullying seriously. Gone are the days when you spent six hours a day confined to the schoolyard trying to avoid your tormentors. Society has come around to the notion that a school should be a safe place that protects children as it educates them.

So what do you do if your preciousness comes to you with tears in her eyes and fear in her heart because an obnoxious bully has focused his attention on her? The first step is to talk to your child. Get the details of what happened, then convey to her that it is not acceptable, nor is it her fault. Let her know that she does not deserve that treatment, that no one ever has the right to abuse her.

This would include being hit, kicked, pushed, threatened, shoved, tripped, spit on, laughed at, or made fun of in person or on Facebook.

What if your child sadly sighs that her persecutor's taunts are accurate? What if your child is overweight? What if your child does need extra help in math? What if your child is 'different'? This is the time to soothe and console your child. Then help her refocus on her strengths: is she kind, funny, smart? Does she value people and friendship? Does she work hard? Is she puppy dog loyal? Whatever it is that makes your child the wonderful, unique person she is, remind her and then tell her that it doesn't matter if she is overweight, different, or needs the extra help. These traits do not define our character, nor who we are. We don't ever have to endure someone's cruelty. We don't ever have to tolerate abuse from anyone. In our house, we call this 'claiming your space on the planet.' Your child is just as vital, and their opinion is just as valid as everyone else's. We all, including our children, have the same right to kindness, joy, love, acceptance, and peace.

I am not advising that your child stand up in the lunchroom and scream that she has had enough. She doesn't have to demonstrate that level of courage, because she has an advocate: you. This brings us to the second step, your child's school. This is where you begin your advocacy by talking to your child's teacher. I prefer to do this task in person, believing that I will get the teacher's undivided attention, but you can call or email if necessary. Don't fool around—do it as soon as you learn of the bullying. The sooner you chat with the school, the sooner you can put a stop to the bullying. By not procrastinating, you will minimize the damage to your child's self-worth, which doesn't need to take any more hits than it already has.

Ask your child's teacher what he or she recommends. What are the school district's policies regarding bullying? How can they ensure the well-being of your child in every educational setting: the cafeteria, the bathroom, the bus line, the playground, after school sports? Ask your teacher to notify anyone who has responsibility for your child (for example: the physical education teacher, the librarian, the bus driver, the playground attendants, the sports coach, the vice principal, and the principal) of the bullying behavior.

After that conversation, I suggest sending an email thanking those involved for their immediate response and cooperation in solving this issue. Use this email to restate the recommendations and steps you agreed upon together, thus documenting your conversation. This documentation is the beginning of the paper trail that will light the fire of importance under the school district's ass if it doesn't step up and protect your child. If the situation is not resolved in a timely, consistent way, you can take your email copy to the principal. Ask for clarification as to why this hasn't been resolved, and who is responsible. Be calm and respectful, even if it's difficult and you're quite justifiably angry. Ask the principal who you can call to report the delinquency in protecting your child. What is the next step in the hierarchy of the school? Would that be the district, the school board, the superintendent? Find out, preferably from the principal herself, how your district is structured. After she assures you that she will handle the issue, send her a detailed email thanking her for her immediate response and cooperation. Document, document, and furthermore, document.

If that fails to rectify the bully's behavior, then follow through with the steps the principal outlined for you. Hit every rung on that ladder, quietly if you can, loudly if you must, recording every step along the way by sending a detailed email thanking the persons you contact for their immediate response and cooperation. You shouldn't have to remind the district that we live in a country that has laws that protect us from abuse, but if you must, do so. If need be, remind the district that you have ample documentation of your diligent, polite, proactive efforts to help district employees protect your child's emotional and physical well-being. Some people are glad to do their jobs. Others really don't want to, and won't do them at all unless you make it so that the consequences of not doing the job are far more undesirable than just stepping up and putting a stop to bullying behavior.

The final step is to explain the above process to your child. Explain the legalities of our system. I did this by making some popcorn and sitting my munchkins down for a viewing of reality court TV. It doesn't really matter what judge/court shows you watch. They all are a great visual manifestation of our legal system. They demonstrate that you cannot do whatever you want to others, just because you want to. If you hit someone, they can sue you for damages. If you harass someone, they can get a restraining order. I explained to my young jury panel that only in school do people allow someone to bully them, then feel ashamed for telling someone. When you grow up and someone is abusive, you tell the police and/or a lawyer, and then a judge. The judge will then lecture them about their anger issues and award you damages. Help your child to understand that no one ever has the right to victimize her. You have the right to stand up and claim your space on the planet.

Only your family can make the determination if self-defense is okay. In our family it is absolutely okay to defend yourself. The self-defense must be an immediate response to the threat of physical violence, not a planned-out brass-knuckled attack. However, the school has certain protocols in place to deal with bullying and violence. Some schools have a zero tolerance policy and reporting the bullying is the child's only option. Running and screaming down the hall or curling up in the fetal position until help arrives, are not options my child would exercise. Therefore, if she chooses to defend herself she would be subject to the school's disciplinary measures, but she would not receive any discipline from us. Of course, if we were to reach the distressing conclusion that it wasn't self-defense, then her punishment would be swift and severe.

CHAPTER TWENTY-TWO:

SKIPPING SCHOOL

SKIPPING SCHOOL

School is not optional. This is nonnegotiable. Education is the path to a better life, for all of us, especially our children. If your children are skipping school and you do nothing about it, you are failing them. The parent who bellyaches, "But I can't make him!" is talking bullshit. You need to do whatever it takes to give your child an education. It is your obligation.

From the very beginning of the educational process, you need to acknowledge the good grades and the efforts of your children. I use the word 'efforts' for a good reason. I don't care if the child writes his letters like a three-fingered chimpanzee; his efforts need praise. You must constantly reinforce how proud you are of the effort your child puts in. My oldest could draw like a little Picasso, so his pictures were easy to display on the fridge. My youngest wasn't quite as talented. We learned, of necessity, to ask him to describe his pictures to us before we made assumptions. However, we still displayed those pictures prominently beside Picasso's on our fridge. He may not be a famous artist one day, but he will always know that we respected his efforts.

An adult's attitude about the importance of education is what will ingrain that value in a child. The home dialogue about education can never end. Children must know that an education is the only path to success. If you have an education, you don't have to be poor, hungry, cold or dependent on someone else. I apologize in advance to all of you who are spinning the $5.00 pizza signs. When we pass you on the street corner, my littlest will proclaim, "He didn't get an education!" I have conditioned him to believe that if he doesn't go to school, spinning a pizza sign will be the best he can hope for. Misleading? Maybe a little. Maybe somewhere out there is a sign spinning wizard with a master's degree who gets so much fulfillment from spinning the sign that he just can't tear himself away from the sign spinning trade.

Uh, yeah.

It's best to set the bar high, starting by making sure your child does his homework. When your child comes home from school, even in kindergarten, make him sit at the table and do some work. Five minutes of reading, writing, or math. If your six-year-old's teacher doesn't send homework home, create your own. You're trying to establish a habit and an expectation: homework is the first thing that happens when they get home. Then they can play. If you start this from the beginning of the educational process, you won't have to fight so hard when they turn into teenagers.

Set the right standard and don't waver. If your child plays sports or does other extra-curricular activities, she must maintain good grades and do her homework. Don't wait until middle school, when the school district mandates this policy. If your little guy or girl plays for the YMCA, if you're involved in the youth soccer program, if you have a future karate champion in your midst...hell, if your kid wants to swim in the backyard pool, she must do her schoolwork first. If she doesn't do it, then she doesn't play. I don't care if the coach calls you. She didn't do her schoolwork, so she doesn't play.

From the time your child is little you can and should encourage your child's career interests, whatever they may be, by making a plan. Show them how a person becomes a doctor, a dentist, or a plumber. When my daughter was younger she wanted to be a cosmetologist, so we mapped out everything it would take to become a cosmetologist. We talked with cosmetologists. We investigated cosmetology schools. Then she changed her mind and decided she wanted to be a pilot so we navigated that field. I would encourage you to look into your community for resources. There are clubs for young would-be pilots. There are clubs for future police officers or firefighters. High schools are loaded with resources. Even if your child isn't in high school yet, you can call your local school for information. Your child is not too young for all this information. If your child is ten and wants to be an architect, help him view that world, and keep it in focus. It is too daunting a task for a child to turn a dream into a reality without a lot of guidance and help from his grownups.

Here is where it gets a little tricky. Should you reward your kids for their grades? I say: definitely! Many people don't agree with me. I don't care what parents use to motivate their kids about school, as long as the motivation works. In addition to the monetary reward/punishment system for grades, we use their cell phones to keep them on track. For us, a teenager's cell phone is like having a goose that lays golden eggs. If my child maintains good grades, I will pay for his cell phone plan. However, if my child cannot seem to maintain good grades, he certainly does not need the distraction of a cell phone.

Some kids, like my littlest, struggle in school. Things did not come easy for him. He has had some minor health problems that made matters worse. Sometimes he would get frustrated and think that he couldn't do it. I would hug his little body, and tell him that I understood it was tough. Then I would sit him down, stare into his bright blue eyes, and tell him he could do anything. It might take more work from him, but he could do anything anyone else could do, if he was willing to work at it. Laziness is what stops you from reaching your goals. He could accomplish amazing things if he understood how to work hard for what he wanted. He may have needed physical therapy to learn the basics of skipping, and sometimes it sort of looked like galloping, but he was so proud of himself when he could finally skip/gallop around our living room. That pride was well earned. He worked hard for it.

Thus we come to skipping school. Parents who have trouble with their kids skipping school amaze me. Skipping school is not an option. I don't have to worry about this issue with my little scholars, because they understand how serious we are about education. I dealt with the problem in advance by explaining to them that if they ever showed us that they couldn't go to school all by themselves, then their mommy could and would go with them. I would explain to every one of their teachers, in every one of their classes, that they couldn't be trusted to attend school on their own, so I'd have to come with them. In that case, after we rearranged things so I could sit beside my little absentee, I would pull out a Kleenex to wipe their nose. I also mentioned that halfway through the class, I would find it necessary to stand up and exclaim loudly, "Oh, I think he needs to make a poopie!" Skipping class is not a problem for us.

I hope you have noticed that my emphasis here is mostly on education and not simply school. I do not believe that the public school system is the right fit for everyone. Parents have so many opportunities now for educating our children that if your child isn't thriving in the regular school system, I would encourage you to research your options and find other solutions. School isn't the start and end of education, simply a major part of it.

CHAPTER TWENTY-THREE:

SMOKING AND FRIENDS

FRIENDS AND SMOKING

Smoking is gross, smells bad, and could eventually kill you. Perhaps for those reasons, it seems to be immensely popular in junior high and high school. Every day, when I pick my child up, I am amazed at how many young people smoke. Obviously, these children have way too much money. Smoking is expensive. Where does a fourteen-year-old get his money? Usually from the parents. That source would immediately end if I caught my child smoking. I would not give my child a single quarter from that moment forward. If they were going to the movies with their friends, I would go buy them a ticket. If they ran out of lunch money, I would go to the school and prepay for all of their lunches. I would personally dig out all the loose change from my sofa so my little chimney couldn't get a single cigarette from my currency.

"They also get them from their friends," some parents might whine. Let me assure you that that's a fixable problem. Let's talk about friends for a minute. Your child's friends are the best indicator of how well your child is doing. Pay attention to who your kid's friends are, and how well those friends are doing. Are their friends delinquents, always in trouble? Do they think they are too cool for school? Are these the people you want influencing your kid? My friend called me, upset because her delinquent kid got into trouble with his delinquent friends. Again. When she grounded him from those same delinquent friends, he screamed, "You can't pick my friends!" Wanna bet?

I tell my children all the time that I love a good challenge. You'll recall that we talked about how being a grown up gets boring. Sometimes the only challenge I get is how to outsmart my children. What do you do if your kid has wretched little demons for friends? What if they have their nasty little claws deep in your child's hide and are quickly dragging him to hell? You make his friends not want to be friends with him. I may not be able to pick my child's friends, but I can make damn sure they don't pick him.

How could I do this? Easy breezy. I bought a megaphone. I had my kids with me when I bought it. They got all excited thinking of all the ways they could use it. Then my daughter stopped, dread spreading across her face, and asked, "Why are you buying a megaphone?" I explained: "I am going to help you pick good friends." Sometimes being a parent is so much fun. I went on to explain to my children that I could help them pick good people to be friends with. We wanted her to be friends with people who stayed out of trouble, thought school was important, and did not smoke. If she ever reached the incorrect conclusion that her associations were unimportant to us, my new megaphone would help me show her where she was mistaken.

I could make her bad friends not want to be friends with her. I calmly explained: if I picked her up from school and caught her smoking, I would get on my megaphone and inform them that I was the mom of the blonde girl smoking. I would ask them, with my megaphone, who gave my daughter cigarettes. I would follow them into the gas station where they bought the cigarettes and ask, with my megaphone, if they are selling cigarettes to minors. I would follow them around, everywhere, me and my megaphone. Using my megaphone, I would ask her if that butt cream stopped the itch. I would wonder into the megaphone if she still thought that old science teacher was hot. Everywhere she and her friends went, I would follow. I would loudly proclaim that smoking is about as cool as a mom with a megaphone. Then I asked my precious girl, "How long do you think your friends would want to be friends with you, if they knew your mom had a megaphone like mine?

CHAPTER TWENTY-FOUR:

SEX, DRUGS, AND ROCK-N-ROLL

SEX, DRUGS, AND ROCK-N-ROLL

Reading this far, you have surely noticed the consistent message of teaching our children from the earliest of ages. We can see the direct connection between the small things we teach them as small children and the bigger lessons that will prepare them for life. Let us move onto a big and rather scary group of issues: sex, drugs, and rock-n-roll!

First, drugs and alcohol. (Some parents may yearn for them at the very thought of the whole subject). Denial Island is a wonderful paradise, in which your precious tropical flower would never do drugs or alcohol. Reality: Denial Island is a fictitious place, created by lies—lies to yourself about your child, and perhaps lies to your child as well. In this instance, lying does not serve us as parents. Kids have talked to their peers. They know about drugs and alcohol. How much detail you disclose to your child is up to you, but remember that our children can smell bullshit a mile away. They know when we are lying and they lose respect for us. You don't have to convince them that they were conceived by immaculate conception but can omit to what degree you participated in drugs, alcohol, and sex. For myself and my girl, I didn't want to lie and undermine the trust I want us to have, so I told her the truth. Yes, I did do some drugs when I was younger, while omitting most of the particulars. When she asked what it was like, I told her that they say "getting high" for a reason. I also informed her that drugs and alcohol were dangerous, illegal, and would not be tolerated in our home. I described how it went when I was growing up, when my parents didn't really care about me. While I am sure that they loved me, they didn't care enough about me to stop me. They liked Denial Island, where life was easy for them, and where I wasn't important enough to fight for. Then I told her that her situation was different. Being the luckiest of girls, she had a mom and a dad who would do whatever it took to keep her away from drugs and alcohol. I burnt my visa to Denial Island.

I went on to explain to my daughter that if she got caught doing drugs, I would call the cops and have her arrested. If she wanted to experience the realities and consequences of getting high, that could be arranged, and better if it happened before age eighteen, before it went on her permanent record. I wanted her to be scared enough to decide that getting high was not worth it, before addiction set in, before learning that being arrested is just the price you pay for the high you're chasing.

Don't freak out here because you have watched too many Lifetime movies. Your little drug fiend won't wind up in the back room of a backwoods police department. In the state where we live (call your local police department to verify their procedures) it is a misdemeanor. That means that your pre-addict will be arrested, booked, and released all in the same day. You will be lucky if your little pre-addict goes to juvenile hall, not that I think you should volunteer that bit of information. In fact, I would lead the conversation in the opposite way, implying that they may even do strip searches to juveniles. I would wonder aloud if peeing in front of a group of strangers was always embarrassing, or if one eventually got used to it.

I also explained that she would have to snitch on all of her buddies. We would need to know where she got the drugs or the alcohol, so we could have the suppliers arrested. We would need to know who she was with, so we could inform their parents, who could have their kids arrested in turn. Why not experience the realities of druggie life together? Then I wondered out loud if her friends would still want to be her friends after that. I wondered if it would be awkward at school.

It wasn't over. I explained with some maternal glee that I would also become her new BFF. We wouldn't go anywhere without each other. If she wanted to go shopping with her friends (the ones who were not caught doing illegal activities), I would have to come along. If she had a school activity like a football game, we would sit together. She would even get to come with me to my massage. Maybe the massage therapist would let her rub my feet. If I could not trust her to make the right and legal decisions on her own, I would hold her hand until she grew up a bit. When she could show me how mature and adult-like she had become, we'd revisit this.

Any parents who let the kids smoke a little weed at their house should probably hope none of the kids has a parent like me. I believe it's perfectly reasonable, and good parenting, to have a massive reaction to this. If other parents gave my child drugs or alcohol, I'd let the police know so that they could investigate and verify if they were contributing to the delinquency of a minor. I don't care if my kid thinks they are the coolest parents ever. I do not care if they think it's normal to experiment, and just want to confine it to the safety of their home. It is not any other parent's place to decide what is right for your child. If they assert that right to themselves, you have every right to go to the wall reasserting your own parental rights. I will, if need be. I hope you'll do the same. This is not a debate about whether or not pot should be legal. In most places, right now, it happens to be illegal, which means that using it can get one in serious trouble. This is about right and wrong: legal and illegal. This is about making the very best decisions for our kids at all times. This is also about the dangers of drugs, and that for some people, even once is too much. Some people's bodies instantly recognize alcohol, responding to that first drink and wanting it again. An alcoholic I know describes that first drink as this warmth that spreads throughout your body. Moreover, whether or not pot is itself addictive, very few heroin addicts started with heroin. For the majority of users, it starts with marijuana. Even if they do not become addicted, alcohol and drugs inhibit our decision making abilities. Sometimes even once is too much. Do you want to be responsible for that one time, or do you want to know that you did everything imaginable to stop your child from becoming another statistic?

Moving onward, who wants to talk about sex? What's the matter? Are you nervous all of a sudden? Are your palms sweaty? Do you feel a little lightheaded? You don't want to think about your precious little girl having intercourse yet? Yeah, me neither. But...no Denial Island for us, remember? This is going to be scary and uncomfortable for you, as well as disappointing, because: teenagers are having more sex than you are! If you're completely confident that your child isn't already getting freaky, I can guarantee you that their peers are. Your children spend the majority of their time with these sexually active kids. At this point in their life, sex is the biggest thing that is going to happen (or is already happening) to them, so you need to talk to them about it.

Do you believe in abstinence? You want your precious little guy to wait until he says his vows before friends, family, and God, on his wedding day? Awesome. That's so cool. The problem is this: your precious little guy has an overwhelming urge to…well, remember your own teen years and use your imagination. It is far more important for your child to be informed, protected, and childless, than to be abstinent. So ask your kid, without judgment, without consequences: what does he believe? Does he want to wait until his wedding day, or does he want to sample some fruit before he makes a pie? Then give him the information and the tools to be informed, protected, and baby-free.

I am not asking you to help your child have sex. I am making the case that, here as in other sensitive matters, Denial Island is no refuge. In fact, it will harm your child and their future. We have to be honest. Your child's biggest source of information is his or her peers. Let us imagine that you raised him to believe in abstinence, drilled this into his head every single Sunday since he was two. Now suppose he's considering 'doing it' with some girl. Do you really want him to ask the quarterback for pointers, because he knows that coming to you would cause you to have a complete freak out? Maybe you can accept that he has his own opinions and beliefs on the issue. Wouldn't you rather have him protected and informed vs. paying child support at the age of sixteen?

I am not condoning teenage sex. I am saying, however, that the discussion must be had, and that you are a safer source of information than the all-conference quarterback. It enables you to share that information, so that the future you wish for them is the future they can have.

Now that you have informed your child, if you want to make the unwise choice all but impossible, you can set some limits. For example, no alone time. None! Your child and her boyfriend do not need to be alone. Nearly everyone would rather be alone to have sex. If you do not allow them to be in the bedroom alone (they can do homework with the door open or even in the living room) they cannot have sex. If you do not run to the grocery store for milk and leave them alone, they cannot have sex. If you do not take a bath while they watch TV alone, they cannot have sex. Just don't leave them alone. Ever. We have friends who went camping. Their precious fifteen-year-old didn't want to go, so they left her alone. Guess who she had over? They were shocked when she turned up pregnant. Teenagers are stupid. They are full of hormones. If you don't want them getting it on, they should never be left alone with the opposite sex.

Let's say you do everything right. You don't take camping trips, you don't go to the store, you don't even nap on the couch when your teenager's 'friend' is over. When your child complains that her boyfriend's parents "trust" them, and whines that you are mean because you do not, you even stop letting her go over to their house. Even when you do everything you can to deter alone time, your teenager will still find ways to have sex. That's why giving them the information and protection they need is vital.

Sexual orientation doesn't change any of this. All of the above guidelines apply to your child: straight, gay, transgender, or just generally confused. Even if you walk solidly on the heterosexual path, I hope you can accept that the gender of whom your child eventually loves is simply none of your business. If we support our children, cherish them, and love them unconditionally, then hopefully our children will grow up to pick healthy partners, who will support them, cherish them, and love them unconditionally. That is the best we can hope for.

I almost forgot about rock-n-roll. Unless your child is listening to cult crap filled with lyrics about cop killings, don't hyperventilate over what music they listen to. If music corrupts our souls, then why am I writing a book about responsible parenting, and why are you reading it? We were all young once too. Our parents hated our music. It is normal for teens to like all music that rattles and offends their parents. Just tell them to turn that crap down and don't worry about it. If the video they watch is too pornographic, turn it off. If they want to dress like the newest slut star, tell them no. If they buy the cult crap, throw it out. Focus the majority of your energy on drugs, alcohol, and sex; let them win the rock-n-roll fight, which is by far the least damaging. They will eventually outgrow that crap. You did.

CHAPTER TWENTY-FIVE:

MENDING FENCES

MENDING FENCES

Let's say that your grown child has barely embarked into the voyage of adulthood, or maybe she is well into middle life, but her counselor has sent her to you to air out her pain. Your child is at a mature point in her life and wants to have an honest reconciliation, but it feels as if she has returned to point out all your deficiencies. You are burdened with overflowing buckets of guilt. What now? I know that it is the toughest thing to make amends to the people that you love unendingly and sacrificed so much for. I'm not trying to add to your burden, but to help you unload it. I've had to. There are days when I don't reach the goal, when I miss the standard, when I am impatient, and when I'm tired. Sometimes I make the wrong choice. Sometimes I am selfish and even take care of my own needs first (gasp!). This doesn't make me a bad parent; it makes me human, as are you. But being human does not excuse our failings. We have to take responsibility for those. We have to acknowledge how we failed and how it made our children feel. We have to strive to do better and not repeat the behavior that hurt them, just as we expect of our kids. In order to have healthy relationships with our children, especially as they become adults, we have to make amends.

Here I place all responsibility on the parent. We have to be held to the higher standard because we are older. Okay, so he's eighteen. I know that you want to say that he is all grown up now, but he isn't. You are always going to be older, with more life experience to pull from. Our children act on impulses and thoughts from developing brains, which causes a whole spectrum of problems. They may say and do things that make us feel horrible. I believe that we must let go of our bitternesses as parents. Grudge holding will be poisonous to the relationships we want to have with our grown children. Whatever your kid said to you when he was ten, thirteen, or even twenty, even if it broke your heart, let it go. Cry if you must, but then let go of it. Remind yourself that you are not a perfect person, just as your children aren't.

So how does a woeful, apologetic parent mend the fissures in the parent/child relationship? The first step in the absolution process is to listen to your child's issues without offering up any excuses. Don't tell her that you did the best you could (even if true), because it's an excuse and therefore is irrelevant. If your child is coming to you with pain in her heart, then your best wasn't good enough. Don't justify yourself or your behavior. What you did, or why, doesn't really matter if it harmed your child emotionally, mentally, or physically.

Don't pass the blame around. How your own parents treated you is not merely irrelevant, but is the worst excuse of all. If you saw them make the mistake, you had every opportunity to watch out for it and every duty not to repeat it, right? You can't blame your present spouse or partner, or even your ex. If you fell short, it was most likely because you looked out for the child's interests second, or last, rather than first.

After you have listened, without offering up any excuses, apologize. Acknowledge what she is saying and how it hurt her. Maybe you don't remember it the way she says it happened; doesn't matter. Her perception is what matters. If she perceives that something was painful, then it was painful for her. I believe it's better to be wrong than to damage your relationship with your child. I'll take being wrong if it means taking the pain away from my child. I can live with being wrong; I can't live with becoming emotionally severed from my child.

After you have offered up a heartfelt apology, you can ask your child what you can do. Maybe your apology is enough, but maybe it isn't. Admit you were wrong and ask your child for guidance. Sometimes we do things that destroy trust, and that takes time to heal. Respect her limits and boundaries. Ask your child what she would need you to do for her to truly understand your depth of love and sorrow. Then do it. Be diligent in your promises. Live your life in such a way that displays your efforts to rebuild both trust and love, and that will help foster an environment where forgiveness can grow.

Try to keep in mind that the adult relationships we eventually want to have with our children are never mandatory, they are a blessing and a privilege. We only earn this privilege by acknowledging our child's truths, respecting her differences, and by allowing the parent/child relationship to evolve and change.

CHAPTER TWENTY-SIX:

PARENTHOOD IS A MARATHON

PARENTHOOD IS A MARATHON

Hey, we're almost done! Kind of a short book, wasn't it? At least compared to the long part of our lives we spend raising our children. Well, I told you at the onset that it wasn't rocket science. If you apply these principles regularly, you will see a drastic difference in the behavior of your children. Here's the real secret to why these concepts work: if you convince your children that you would do any, or all, of the things I suggest, you will see your children's behavior change. I have not had to take a megaphone to school and yell at my girl for smoking, because she believes that I would do it. My children think that their mom is slightly crazy. This idea was easy for me to cultivate, because confrontation doesn't bother me. I don't care about what other people think and neither should you. Your first and only priority is your child. It doesn't matter what other people think. It can't matter what other people think.

Years ago, my best friend and I loaded up our kids, five total, and went swimsuit shopping. Finding a swimsuit was dreadful, but the kids were fantastic. My friend and I would take turns in the dressing room while the other one waited with the kids. These kids were patient. They didn't rile each other up. They critiqued our suits and even helped vote on which suits looked the best. My friend was trying on one last suit, so I told our wonderfully well-behaved fashion judges that, because of their wonderful behavior, we would stop and get them ice cream on our way home. Out of nowhere, this woman approaches me and makes a nasty comment about how she never had to bribe her children. Seriously? Who does that? Anyway, I calmly informed her that her opinion didn't mean shit to me, and furthermore, I was amazed that she thought enough of herself to even consider that I would care about her or her kids. I was disappointed when she scurried off, because I was fully prepared to start a loud lesson for my little fashionistas about rudeness from perfect strangers.

Hopefully, your expectations are now more realistic. You understand that children are naughty because growing up is a learning process. This deeper understanding will help you not take the parenting process too personally. Your identity need not be tied up in how well-behaved your children are, how good they are in sports, or how well they do in school. Understanding these principles will help you to be more consistent. You've made the connection that being consistent is vital to changing your child's behavior. The importance of consistent follow-through will teach your child self-control, as you now understand that self-control is at the core of becoming a successful adult. You can now start teaching them to respect themselves, other people, and property. You have a deeper understanding of how toxic favoritism is, and how it will erode the relationships within your family.

The last element to add is an abundance of positive reinforcement and unconditional love, while being mindful that you are creating a human being. Remember, people, they may be children today, but one day your children are going to grow up. When they do, they are going to hold you accountable. Think about that for a minute. You are going to have to answer for any crap you pulled: alcoholism, drugs, mental or physical abuse, neglect, favoritism, or even choosing your new girlfriend or boyfriend over them. Those are the big things, the unforgivable things. I hope that if you're reading this book, alcohol, drugs or abuse are not even a consideration in the development of your children's lives. Because, and many of you know it from your own upbringings, even without those acutely damaging acts, your children will come back to you one day and hold you accountable for the ways that you failed them. Your actions today have an impact well into the future. To lose sight of that reality is a major mistake. That is why affection and love are essential for our children. If your children always feel loved by you, they will forgive a multitude of failings: the times we were impatient. The times we were insensitive. The times we were selfish. All those times we were human.

Now that we have reviewed the concepts of effective parenting, and the importance of unconditional love, I want to remind you to maintain a continuous dialogue with your little people. Talk constantly with your kids. Talk about everything. Take every opportunity to teach them. My twelve-year-old daughter was with me one day when I stopped for gas. As I was waiting for the tank to fill, a man next to us was verbally abusing his wife/girlfriend. He was calling her a dumb bitch, telling her she was stupid. While leaning against the trunk of our car, I explained to my baby chick that what he was doing to his girlfriend/wife was verbal abuse. I explained that I would rather be alone than tolerate that kind of treatment from someone who professed to love me. I went even further, saying how sad her parents must be to know that she chooses to spend her life with someone so awful. We talked about how we teach people how to treat us, and that I was absolutely positive that the poor girl could find someone else to be with. I made no effort to prevent him from overhearing.

Did it stop the abusive asshole from being an abusive asshole? Maybe it did for that moment, but probably not permanently. It did, however, show my daughter that it was a choice, and that she could choose better. I could have ignored his disrespectful display at the gas station, but I might not get another chance for my daughter to see authentic verbal abuse first hand. You don't have to be as vocal as I am to make the point; my daughter and I could have talked inside our car. I chose to try to make him feel like a jackass. You don't have to do it my way, as long as you do it. Take every opportunity for dialogue because it may change the outcome for your kids.

Parenting is like running a marathon. It isn't pretty. Think about it. Marathon runners are all sweaty and nasty. They get up every day at some ungodly hour and run. Rain, snow, wind; nothing stops them. They don't show up for their 26.2 mile race in full makeup and high heels. Their hair looks like crap. Their clothes are ugly. Sometimes they even vomit in public at the end of the race. More importantly, while they are doing it, they don't care that you think they're batshit crazy. That's parenthood. It is a test of endurance, patience, humiliation, and dedication. If you stop caring about what other people think, then you will be a more effective parent. If it doesn't matter to you what the neighbors, the teachers, or even the other parishioners in your church think, you will be free to implement parenting methods that work even if they're unconventional. Stop worrying about everyone else. Do what is effective for your family and for your kids.

Parenting is a long, hard, thankless job. We have to find ways of coping. I encourage you to try out the methods in this book, modify them, and use them consistently to fit into your circumstances and family. I also hope you have a well developed sense of humor, because your sense of humor is the best tool you have to help you run the parenthood marathon.

Oh, and don't worry if you throw up a few times along the route, that's normal.

About the Author

Shannon D. Jackson is the mother of three children, two boys and one girl. She and her family live in the Pacific Northwest.

She channeled the exhaustion that comes from the sheer duration of parenting into humorous, innovative, and effective parenting techniques.

Out of frustration at the way we judge ourselves and each other throughout the parenting journey, and motivated by the lack of support she saw from fellow parents, she compiled her experiences into a candid and witty parenting book.